EVERYTHING ANIMAL REIKI

A Simple Guide to Meditating with Animals for Healing

KATHLEEN PRASAD

Published in the United States by
Amazon

ISBN-13:978-1512027990
ISBN-10:1512027995

Production: Leah D'Ambrosio
Cover design: Sheryl Schlameuss
Front and back cover photographs: Kathleen Prasad
  (www.animalreikisource.com)
Interior photographs: Lexie Cataldo (www.injoyphotography.com)
  pp. 33 and 135
Calligraphy: Hiroko Sasanuki

Distributed by Amazon

DISCLAIMER: The suggestions in this book are not intended as a substitute for professional veterinary care. Reiki sessions are given for the purpose of stress reduction and relaxation to promote healing. Reiki is not a substitute for medical diagnosis and treatment. Reiki practitioners do not diagnose conditions nor do they prescribe, perform medical treatment, nor interfere with the treatment of a licensed medical professional. It is recommended that animals be taken to a licensed veterinarian or licensed health care professional for any ailment they have.

*For all the animals in my life who have honored me
with their healing presence*

TABLE OF CONTENTS

TABLE OF CONTENTS

CHAPTER ONE

WHAT IS REIKI?

There are so many reasons to love Reiki for animals! Those of us who have been practicing for a long time (or even a short time) know this well. Animal Reiki cleverly unifies the practices of healing touch, animal connections and meditation to create balance, harmony and healing. Reiki is quite a simple practice, and in this book, I will guide you through a down-to-earth explanation of Reiki's meaning, the basics of system of practice, treatment guidelines for sharing Reiki with people and animals, as well as share over 30 meditation practices to help you get started in supporting your animals today!

The Word

Rei means "spirit," and Ki means "energy," so literally, the word "Reiki" translates as "spiritual energy." What is this spiritual energy? My teacher Frans Stiene has a wonderful answer:

> *From a traditional Japanese perspective we can say*
> *that Reiki means our True Self, and the system of Reiki*
> *(Usui Reiki Ryoho) is a system that helps us to*
> *remember our True Self/Reiki again.*

The practices of Reiki, many of which I will share with you in this book, are designed to help you to reawaken your inner wisdom and compassion, your inner power and healing abilities so that you can bring yourself back to balance and your "True Self" again. When we can do this for ourselves, we can also help our animals!

Reiki as a Meditative Practice

Reiki is a meditative system of spiritual practice created by Mikao Usui in early 20th century Japan. The system of Reiki utilizes several elements that nurture balance and wellness:

> The Reiki Precepts
> Visualization Practices
> Hands-on Practice for the Self and Others
> Symbols and Mantras
> Initiations/Reiju/Attunements

If we take a deeper look at each of these elements, we can see the heart is to create a meditative state of mind for healing. When working with the precepts, the key is to contemplate them in a meditative way so that we can go deeper into their meaning and purpose in our everyday lives, bringing change and healing to all that we do. When working with the visualization practices, the key is to follow the breath into a meditative space where healing can happen. As a practitioner, when we offer a healing session to a person or animal, the key is that we go deeper into a meditative state of mind so that we can compassionately support the healing process. When practicing the symbols and mantras, either through contemplation or chanting, this helps us to release our busy mind and find our inner "still point" —or inner meditative space to facilitate healing. Finally, as a teacher, when offering initiations to our students, the key is to create a compassionate meditative space within us and within the ritual to support the student's healing process.

In reality, Reiki simply offers simple practices to remember that we are all connected in the web of life; thus, Reiki nurtures compassion, within ourselves for our own healing, and for the support of others. Both teachers and practitioners of the system of Reiki often describe how their meditation practice has changed their lives—from the inside out— and made their world a better and more peaceful, compassionate place.

Thus we can see that every part of the system of Reiki is ultimately about meditation and compassion as keys to healing.

Ways to Meditate

There are many meditations included in this book, and each of them can be done in several ways. The meditations are meant to help you to bring peacefulness to every moment in your life, not just while you are alone, eyes shut and meditating at home. Each of these meditations can build one upon the other. For example, it is easiest to sit with eyes closed to get into the meditative space, however in time you will be able to stand with eyes open, and finally to find that same peaceful space even while you are walking your dog. To really test your meditation stamina, try meditating in the kennel of an animal shelter! Be creative and find ways to include animals in your practice.

Spending time with animals while we are meditating can help us develop our own sensitivities. Animals are wonderful models for us since they authentically embody so many spiritual qualities throughout their lives and even as they face death. Sharing meditation with animals can help guide us toward being better people and creating a healthier planet, one where people nurture wellness through the practice of compassion and a life of joyful service to others.

Following are the three great ways to meditate:

1) **Sitting meditation.** For this type of meditation, where you are sitting still with your eyes open and/or closed (as you prefer), you may want to purchase a meditation bench (I recommend meditationbench.com for a great selection!). It is also great to create a sacred, quiet space in your home where you can go and sit. Place your bench in front of objects that are special to you: photos of loved ones, statues or crystals that have special meaning to you, a vase of flowers, a candle, incense, quiet music, etc. When you sit down to do a formal meditation, all these special items can help support you in going deeper into your inner space.

2) **Standing meditation**. For this meditation, find a peaceful place in nature (or with your horse or other outdoor animal) to stand and connect deeply with the earth. You will find the natural elements naturally nurture the quiet space inside of you.

3) **Walking meditation.** For this meditation, find a place to walk that is fairly quiet so that you can focus on the nature around you. If you are walking your dog, imagine you are connected by your hearts, not by the leash. While you are practicing this meditation, if you are alone, allow yourself to embrace nature all around you. If you are with your dog, you can also notice your dog's focus and delight in each moment.

Uses

Practicing the techniques of Reiki supports balance and harmony on all levels. Using Reiki maintains health, heals illnesses and injuries on all levels, and can ease the transition between life and death. Healing doesn't necessarily mean physical cure; healing could mean a spiritual rebalancing during the body's transition. Reiki is about peeling back the layers of our lives to rediscover our true nature of connection with all things.

> *When we learn to relax and simply be present for the animal without judgment, we will find it much easier to connect with animals, and in turn, we will begin to see better responses from them.* -Kathleen Prasad, *Reiki for Dogs*

CHAPTER TWO

WHY REIKI IS IDEAL FOR USE WITH ANIMALS

Reiki is a wonderful complement to your animal's health and wellness program, since it works safely with all other forms of healing, both allopathic and holistic.

- The essence of Reiki is its simplicity. Reiki needs only two key ingredients: your intention and the animal's acceptance.

- Reiki can effectively address any problem an animal may face: physical, mental, emotional or spiritual.

- Reiki is gentle and noninvasive, yet powerful.

- Reiki will heal the origin of the problem, even if it is not known. You do not need to diagnose (nor is this your role as practitioner).

- Reiki can also heal the situation. Its nature is to bring healing and balance and this happens on the levels of the individual and beyond.

- Reiki is just as effective from a short distance as it is hands-on. Thus, animals can choose to receive each treatment in the ways most comfortable for them.

- Reiki can do no harm; you can't "do it wrong."

- You can't "overdo" Reiki. Reiki will not give more healing and/or energy to the animal than he or she is open to receive.

- Reiki always heals on some level, even if you don't see an outward solution to the animal's problem.

By simply relaxing, being quiet, breathing and having a heartfelt intention to help another being, you create a sacred space. In this space, all things are possible.

CHAPTER THREE

PHYSICAL, EMOTIONAL AND SPIRITUAL HEALING WITH REIKI

A Story of Physical Healing

There was a kitten one day in the shelter where I was volunteering. He had been poisoned. His mother had somehow ingested poison and then the babies had nursed, and so there were three kittens and the mom. By the time I got there, two of the kittens and the mom had already died and there was this one kitten left, and he was in pretty bad shape. He was very listless and couldn't open his eyes. He couldn't stand up and was just lying there. The staff person said to me, "Well, we're not sure he's going to make it, but we want to give him a little time; can you sit and do Reiki?"

So I sat outside the little cage, and after several minutes, the kitten tried to open his eyes and tried to move his head, and he leaned forward, and I could see he saw, he knew. He could sense I was there because, of course, animals are much more sensitive than people, and he was asking for more healing. So I opened the cage door. I put my hands in. I cupped my hands around him and he leaned his little tiny head on the side of my hand, and he was tiny enough that I could easily fit him just within my hands (and I have very small hands). He was just a teeny, tiny little thing. He curled right up and leaned his little head against me and slept.

After about 45 minutes, he woke up. I moved my hands away. He opened his eyes and looked right at me with his very bright eyes, meowed a teeny, little meow, stretched, and went over and drank water.

Amazing, and with just one treatment of 45 minutes! It was literally as if he had come back from the brink of death, with nothing except Reiki.

What is more powerful than being present with an open heart and compassion for another being? Isn't that the ultimate healing? And this is what we do as Reiki practitioners!

This is a beautiful example of how Reiki touches our most inner heart and spreads out in a beautiful ripple effect, and this is why we see these kinds of physical healings, as with the kitten. It is so beautiful to see.

A Story of Emotional Healing

Another day at the shelter when I went in, they asked me to work with a dog who had come in who was very, very ill, but also had been severely abused and was basically shut down. If you've ever seen an animal like this, it's where they are unresponsive; there's just basically "nobody home." He was lying in the back of the kennel, his head down. His eyes were open, but they were glazed over with no expression; he had absolutely no response to people walking through, to all of the loud noise at the shelter. There were dogs barking next to him, and jumping around, but he had absolutely no response. He was completely shut down emotionally.

I sat outside his kennel and I offered Reiki. For me, what this means is, it's really about feeling the love, opening my heart, sitting in compassion and just inviting the animal to share that space. So I sat there for about 45 minutes to an hour. At that time, I had to move on. So I stood up and thanked the dog. I could hardly believe my eyes: as soon as I stood up and thanked him, he got up too. He walked over wagging his tail. He walked up to the front of the kennel, rolled on his back and offered me his tummy, all the while wagging his tail. It was the most amazing transformation from just one treatment.

This healing didn't happen because I was thinking I need to heal this and that problem. It wasn't because I was directing energy to do this and that. It was because an open heart and compassion is the ultimate healer! It doesn't matter how bad something is, Reiki can transform any condition. In essence, Reiki is really love and compassion, and thus it can reach any problem. So I always feel there is always hope, especially because of what I've seen over the years.

Reiki is so powerful, and yet, it is completely non-invasive and very, very gentle.

A Story of Spiritual Healing

Despite the beautiful things I have seen, I know that Reiki is not a cure all. Just because you do Reiki doesn't mean you will never get sick or that you won't die. But over time I have come to realize that it's the peacefulness of Reiki that is really what's important.

There was a dog that came into the shelter one day, and the dog was very vicious and they were going to have to euthanize him. I happened to be there a few hours before that, offering Reiki, and the staff said to me, "Oh, can you at least sit with him? He's very aggressive and nobody can really do anything with him. Maybe it will help somehow?"

I knew that this dog's path had been decided that there was nothing I could do to change it, and yet with Reiki, I knew I could do something.

So I went and sat outside the kennel. I could see that this dog was very vicious and out of his mind with rage. I sat a bit away from the kennel and turned to the side so that I wasn't making him feel even worse (although that would have been hard to do!). He was pacing and snarling. Every person or dog or movement that he saw, he would lunge, snapping and barking.

So I just closed my eyes, went inward, and created that Reiki space. I focused on the peace of Reiki, and just sat. I thought to myself, I'm just going to shine my light, and I hope it helps. I knew that was all I could do. After about 20 minutes, I opened one eye because I could tell things had quieted down. I was afraid to look because he was so sensitive to any movement or any eye contract at all, but I opened one eye just to glance at him. He had actually stopped pacing, stopped barking, stopped growling. He was standing. He would not lie down, but he was standing, leaning against the side of the kennel. His head was down and bobbing up and down slightly because he was falling asleep standing up. Even he could not resist the beautiful power of love and compassion that is Reiki.

Even though he was euthanized later that day, I could feel that his spirit really received a beautiful peacefulness that he otherwise would not have felt in this lifetime. I feel that that was important for his journey. In fact for each and every one of us: it is very, very important to have that peacefulness, even if it is only for a short time. Yes perhaps the dog's life here was ended, but this brief moment of rest for his body, mind and spirit was a profound gift.

Reiki Healing the Situation

What's the ultimate healing of the situation for a shelter animal? They find a home! I've had situations with shelter animals getting adopted immediately after treatments. Sometimes it's with animals that have been there for months, and nobody had looked at them. Yet after a treatment, boom, they are adopted. This happened so much so, that the staff started to talk about it amongst themselves. One time, they even made a bet about a dog that had been there for so long they thought it was hopeless. They wanted me to work with him, and they made a bet as to whether he would get adopted, and sure enough he did, almost immediately.

It doesn't always happen that way, but it often does so I wonder what is going on here. Is it a magical spell? No. I think it's that Reiki uncovers our spirit, so that who we are can shine through. I believe often animals don't get adopted because people can't see who they are. All you can see is stress, fear, upset, or when you look in their faces, there's nobody home. But when we do Reiki, that peacefulness inside comes back. The light in their eyes comes back. The expressions on their faces, and who they really are, shines through again because of that beautiful peacefulness that Reiki brings. And so once we've offered Reiki, now maybe somebody walks by and looks at them, and Wow! They can actually see who they are.

For this reason I wish all Reiki practitioners would volunteer Reiki in their local shelter!

CHAPTER FOUR

THE SYSTEM OF REIKI

All parts system of Reiki, when practiced together, focus on helping us to remember our inner wisdom or "True Self." In Japan, this is known as "Anshin Ritsumei," or enlightenment. When we remember our True Self, we realize that we are deeply connected to one another, and a strong sense of compassion naturally arises. How does this relate to healing? Compassion is the ultimate healing power. Thus, we can see that the true purpose of the system of Reiki is simply to rediscover our inner wisdom and compassion. When we do, profound healing will naturally follow.

The teachings of Reiki include meditating with:

> The Five Precepts
> Hand Positions
> Visualizations such as Joshin Kokyu Ho
> Symbols and Mantras
> Reiju (also called attunements or initiations)

There are three levels in the system of Reiki:

Shoden (Level 1): Japanese meaning, "beginner teachings".

In this level of Reiki the student learns basic Reiki techniques and meditations to begin self-healing as well as helping others. Daily self-practice and practicing with the animals is important to help begin developing an inner energetic quiet and focus, which will support healing of the self and helping others.

Okuden (Level 2): Japanese meaning, "hidden or inner teachings".

In this level of Reiki the student revisits and deepens many concepts begun in Level 1 Reiki, as well as learning the first three Reiki symbols and mantras. Students also learn about "distant healing" practices and with enough experience, can begin charging professionally for services. With daily practice at this level of Reiki, the student will notice a more esoteric and spiritual sense of self-healing and connection to the animals. A deeper awareness of the energetic realm and all things therein begins to arise.

The symbols and mantras help the practitioner to uncover a deeper layer of being, one where we remember that we are all connected in this universe. In this way, they help us to remember oneness and compassion. Compassion is the ultimate healer! The symbols and mantras are not meant to be "given" to another person or animal or to "fix" a particular issue or problem. Each symbol and mantra has a particular meditative focus.

Symbols, Mantras and The Three Secrets

The Japanese spiritual practices of Shingon Buddhism and Mikkyo teach that the ancient wisdom of the Mind, Speech and Body (also known as The Three Secrets) are present everywhere and in all things. It is said that these secrets allow us to uncover our true nature—one that exists both within us and within the entire universe. Historically, practitioners of these systems would use mudras, mantras and visualizations to purify and harmonize The Three Secrets. In the system of Reiki, we can see this reflected in Usui's goal of helping uncover one's true nature. We can also see reflections of The Three Secrets in other Reiki teachings, including the symbols and mantras:

Mind: Reiki visualizations such as the Joshin Kokyu Ho, contemplating the Reiki precepts, and visualizing the symbols help focus the mind.

Body: Reiki "mudras" are present in hands-on healing positions as well as in the Reiju ritual.

Speech: We can see this aspect in the Reiki teachings of speaking or chanting the mantras.

How to Draw the Symbols to Purify Our Mind

- Draw in the air or in your hand with your index finger.
- Draw in the air with your whole hand.

- Draw directly on the body.
- Draw in your mouth with your tongue.
- Draw in the air with the tip of your nose.
- Draw mentally in your mind.

How to Use the Mantras to Purify Our Speech

- Chant them aloud as written or using vowel sounds.
- Repeat them silently in your mind.
- Say them three times as you draw the corresponding symbol.

Shinpiden (Level 3): Japanese meaning, "mystery teachings".

In this level of Reiki the student revisits the teachings and concepts learned in Level 1 and 2 but from an even deeper and more spiritual viewpoint. This level is about developing a state of mind and being—Reiki begins to ripple out into every aspect of your life, not just your practice and meditations. Students learn the fourth symbol and mantra, which supports this spiritual state of mind and being. Students also learn the attunements used when teaching Reiki Levels 1, 2 and 3. When doing daily practice at this level, students will begin to discover their most inner essence, and in so doing, it becomes much easier to connect with the animals.

The most important component of the system of Reiki at any level is one's own daily personal practice, meditation and self-healing. This is the foundation from which all healing experiences with the animals will grow.

Do your practice: Let go of the thoughts and words to just "be" in that indefinable, beautiful healing space every single day. In this way we uncover our true nature and "bright light" and we allow it to manifest in the world.

Our personal practice is what will give us the trust and courage that we need to stay stable, strong, grounded and calm no matter what issues we may face ourselves, or when supporting an animal and his family. The precepts, the symbols and mantras, the meditations, the Reiju: practicing all of these elements supports our ability to connect with the animals through treatments. Similarly, each element of the system of Reiki supports the other elements and helps them function successfully as tools for our self-development, like pieces of a perfect and clever puzzle.

Everyday must be seen as practice. Practice is not about maintaining one's current life-style but about advancing one step at a time. -Mitsunaga Kakudo

CHAPTER FIVE

INTRODUCTION TO REIKI MEDITATION

Reiki is primarily about developing our personal meditation practice because this is the key to going deeper with the animals. It is also your foundation to be able to help yourself and support animals to heal.

Daily practice focuses on developing your inner quiet and focus during your personal meditations and self-healing work. Your daily self-practice is a great time to invite the animals in to share that space and also to see how they help you go deeper into healing.

Self-Healing Shifts

Your daily self-practice will be the foundation for your own healing, and also for your ability to support healing in others. The more you experience the layers of healing within yourself, the easier it will be to trust in the power of Reiki to support others. Reiki can support your physical healing and recovery, create a sense of mental and emotional peace and wellbeing, and help you to connect with your inner essence and being so that you can more easily find and follow your heart's innermost purpose. Reiki will support rebalancing in all layers of your being.

Sometimes as you heal your inner layers, you may feel some discomfort, such as a temporary worsening of symptoms. This "healing response" is something to be grateful for, as it indicates that things long buried are coming to the surface so they can "let go" and you can truly heal. Continuing to practice daily is a great way to help move through any healing response. It's also wonderful to ask a Reiki friend for Reiki support too!

The Reiki Space

While we often hear about the surface practices of Reiki as a "hands-on healing" modality for helping our animals heal bumps and bruises, the deeper teachings of Reiki are about healing of the spirit. Reiki helps us meet our animals' healing challenges with grace and surrender, while we to learn to listen to and be present for them in a compassionate space. It is the cultivation of what I like to call "the Reiki space" –an openhearted mindful "presence" with our animals—that brings with it amazing healing responses.

Reiki starts with you. It is about being able to hold a space of balance within yourself—even in the midst of a chaotic or troublesome situation. How can we do this? Through meditation!

Reiki practices help us learn how to maintain an inner balance and calm at first while we meditate, but in time and with practice, this balance will gradually spread out into a peaceful state of mind in all that we do. I call it the "Reiki ripple effect" —when we open our hearts to balance, clarity and harmony, then healing, contentment, transformation and renewal will follow.

Meditating with the Help of Animals

Learning Reiki for your animals is learning to meditate with your animals for healing.

Because animals are so sensitive to our inner states, when we learn to create an inner state of balance, we can see them almost immediately respond by also becoming calmer and more peaceful. Self-healing (for both ourselves and for our animals) can most easily happen when we are truly at peace. In addition, learning to connect with our animals from this calm inner space will also help our relationship with them to go much deeper.

Do your self-practice on your own, and over time, you will go deeper. But it's much easier with your animals! For example, if you invite your dog or cat to sit with you while you do your practice, or if you stand in the pasture and do your practice with your horse, you're going to go deeper, more quickly. You may also find as you begin to practice on your own, that almost immediately your animals start coming in and wanting to help and share.

When we open up to our animals, when they come forward to share and say, "Oh, okay, you can sit with me," then wow! We will go so much deeper in our practice. Our meditations will be so much quieter. Our minds let go so much quicker. We can feel and sense the energy flowing so much more easily and—this is the kicker—we will probably also feel so much more inspired to do a daily practice because it becomes a part of our animal bonding time. So invite your animals into your meditations! They will support you, inspire you and help you to grow.

Animals as Mirrors and Lights to Our Journey

Animals are wonderful mirrors for our own healing journey. They reflect back to us our own healing strengths and challenges. They are also lights along the path of healing that we take. Some days we may feel that the path is so dark that we don't know which way to go, and then our animals shine their light and we feel encouraged by the love and joy that they radiate so effortlessly. If we open our hearts and listen, it becomes easy to follow their lead in the journey of healing, step by step.

CHAPTER SIX

HUMAN CHAIR PRACTICE

Offering Reiki to a person while she is sitting in a chair is a great and convenient way to offer Reiki. This kind of treatment can be offered in many places, such as in a room in someone's home, in an office at an animal shelter or in a tack room at a barn. Sometimes the experience of Reiki is the best way to explain to a person what Reiki is. The International House of Reiki teaches the human chair treatment as shown here. They are a great way to start, but feel free to use your intuition and let your hands guide you to different positions on or off the body.

The Reiki Touch

All Reiki touch is very gentle, however here are four levels of touch you can choose when offering Reiki. Follow your intuition and you can also ask the person to let you know if they are not comfortable at any time.

1) Light touch: Hands are held flat against the body with light touch.

2) Lighter touch: Only the heel of the hand and the tips of the fingers touch the body.

3) Lightest touch: Only the tips of the fingers touch the body.

4) Aura touch: Hands are positioned just off the body.

Setting Intention

You can help the person you are offering Reiki get into a good state of mind for healing by asking her to relax in the chair, place her hands on her lap where they feel comfortable, close her eyes, set her intention that she is open to heal. As the practitioner, you can start by standing behind them, placing your hands in gassho (palms together in front of your heart) and setting your intention that you are open to hold a beautiful space of healing, balance and harmony to support this person's healing process.

Length of Treatment

Ideally, a treatment will last about thirty minutes, which allows the person to completely relax into the treatment, however even shorter treatments of five to ten minutes can be extremely beneficial.

Hands-on Reiki Chair Sessions

CHAPTER SEVEN

THE REIKI PRECEPTS

The Reiki precepts are guides for living, and one of the main components of the system of Reiki. These precepts are not only the foundation for self-healing in the system of Reiki, but also can be seen deep within all other teachings in the system. It is a powerful practice to simply sit in contemplation with one of the precepts, or to explore the interrelation of the precepts to each other or to other elements of the system of Reiki.

The five Reiki precepts for balanced living, taught by the founder of the system, Mikao Usui, are as follows:

> Just for today ...
> Do not anger
> Do not worry
> Be humble
> Be honest in your work
> Be compassionate to yourself and others

The most important element of Mikao Usui's teachings is resting our mind on the precepts, so that we can lead a life without anger and worry, and therefore we can be humble, honest and compassionate. All the rest of the teachings, (hands on healing, meditations, symbols/mantras, Reiju) are tools to help us to be in that state of mind. -Frans Stiene

I encourage all of you to find an animal shelter or sanctuary near you in which to volunteer Reiki. These animals will be your greatest teachers, and the experience, resolve and strength that you gain in these animal centers will serve you well for any animal Reiki situation you may find yourself in. If we look a bit more closely, we can see that the precepts can be used as guides when working with rescued animals.

1. **Just for today do not anger.** Working with rescued animals can be very difficult when we see the results of past abuse or neglect. We can begin to feel ourselves becoming very angry about how the animal was treated, what he had to go through and so on. This anger at the animal's situation can spiral into anger about the world as a whole and anger toward humanity's treatment of animals in general. Pretty soon we can find ourselves encompassed in a bubble of anger. This anger will merely distract us from our primary goal, which is to help the animal. If we are angry, the animal will sense that and not want to connect with us. If we can focus instead on our desire to help the animal, our anger can be mitigated by our compassion. It can also help us to see the animal with our heart instead of our eyes. If we can see deeper into the very essence and spirit of the animal—see that shining star just waiting to brighten our life—it will be easier to work through any difficulties we face with patience and calm. When we approach our rescued animal with this kind of inner peace, everything will flow toward healing much more easily.

2. **Just for today do not worry.** When working with a rescued animal, we can find ourselves dealing with many health problems. We might rescue an animal suffering with respiratory distress, a skin condition or some physical injury from past abuse or neglect. As we nurture the animal toward healing, we may find ourselves worrying: worrying about other problems that might manifest, about how and if the animal will be able to fully heal from illness and injury and so on. We also might worry about our rescued animal being able to fit into our family, especially if we know the animal has faced difficult and traumatic events in the past. Worrying and fretting about things beyond our control is not helpful for the animal or us. In fact, it is possible that the animal will choose not to connect with us for Reiki when they sense our worry.

If we can again look deeper into the heart and spirit of the animal to see him as already healed, we can help our animal find the hope and courage to get better. We can, for example, see how shiny their coat must have once been, how they would look with proper weight on their bones. We can imagine they are breathing freely and running with strength and vigor across our yard. When we begin to look at our animal for who he really is, he, too, will see us for who we really are, and the relationship can deepen. And in that deepening of trust, the healing of the heart begins. This is where it all starts for the rescued animal—with healing of the heart.

3. **Be humble.** Working with a rescued animal can bring us back into humility. We might have thought initially we were the one doing the "rescuing" —and yet as we create a new and loving relationship with this animal, we might find that our lives are forever changed for the better. We may find our hearts opening more than we had ever thought possible. In working through the healing journey of our rescued animal, we may learn about ourselves and in so doing, find that we are better people for it. And so one day we may realize that it is we who were rescued by this animal. We find ourselves humbled by their capacity to heal and forgive, to let go of the past, and to move forward into a new future with courage, joy and selfless devotion. If only we could learn to live our lives as a rescued animal lives his.

4. **Be honest in your work.** Going through our lives, how often do we ask ourselves, what is our life's work? When we work with a rescued animal, we are helping him to heal, nurturing him physically and emotionally, providing exercise, food and attention, and helping him to build a new beginning as a part of our family. We can realize that it is in this daily practice with him, where we devote ourselves single-mindedly to our task, that we find our heart's true calling. In helping this animal to heal from the past and live his life surrounded in love, we suddenly find that it is in this place that we are being truly honest in our work.

5. **Be compassionate to yourself and others.** Helping a rescued animal is a very compassionate action, which I believe has a ripple effect out into the world. By working with rescued animals in your life, you are not only helping each individual animal, but also making the world a better place by being a model for others. So first and foremost, be kind and gentle to yourself. In following your heart for the animals who need you, you will develop and nurture the compassionate spirit within you.

> *The Five Precepts help us remain mindful about staying balanced in our everyday life. When we practice regularly, it becomes easier to stay balanced when we are working with our animals. A more balanced energy is also more attractive to the animals, so you may notice that the more you work with the precepts, the easier it is to connect with animals—not only your own, but also others with whom you may come into contact. -Kathleen Prasad, Reiki for Dogs*

GUIDELINES FOR TREATMENTS

Before you begin, prepare yourself and the space.

Find a small space the animal is familiar with in which to treat: for example a small room in the house, or the animal's stall in the barn, etc. Allow the animal to move around freely: don't restrain him or her during treatment. Stand nearby, sit on a chair or relax on the floor or a cushion, whatever is most comfortable for you and the animal. Rest your hands on your lap rather than pointing them at the animal. If your muscles are relaxed, the energy will be able to flow freely and you will be able to stay focused easier. Make sure your physical needs have been met so you can remain focused during the treatment (for example, make sure you are fed and hydrated). If you are working with the animal of a friend or family member, have a short discussion about Reiki and what you will be doing so they know what to expect. Make sure they will not be disturbing you or the animal during the treatment. As you greet the animal, behave in a way that inspires trust (quiet, calm voice, still gentle hands, no food or treats).

Allow yourself an undisturbed time duration of 30-60 minutes.

Allow enough time that the animal is able to relax and maybe even fall asleep. You also may go into a deep meditative space. When you or the animal "comes out" of this relaxed place, this is a usual indication that the treatment is over.

Get centered and connected with Reiki through a few moments of meditation or hands-on healing.

Set your intention/ask permission.

Simply ask the animal if he or she would like to receive a Reiki treatment. You can do this by actually saying (in words or in your mind), "Would you like some Reiki today?" or, setting your intention that you will be offering healing in whatever amount he or she is open to (or none at all). Reassure the animal that he or she need take only what Reiki he or she is comfortable with. You will simply be offering healing and it is his or her choice whether and how much to receive.

Focus

To begin the treatment, just intend for the energy to flow freely within your being. Once you have set your intention and focus, let yourself "let go and let Reiki." The stronger the energy flows, the deeper you will find yourself going into a meditative state with a quiet mind and still thoughts. You may find your mind wandering—this is natural. Just take notice of your thoughts if they wander, see them as clouds floating gently by. Then gently bring yourself back to your original intent and focus.

Animals appreciate a passive and open approach.

Do not "beam" or "send" energy to the animal or to a specific health issue the animal has that you "think" needs healing. Instead, try "offering" the energy in a non-assertive manner. Imagine you are creating a Reiki space around yourself, which the animal can move into and out of freely. In this same vein, your body language should match this passive intention: in other words, don't initiate and hold eye contact, don't make yourself "big" and dominant in your body position. For example, try to stay on the same physical level with the animal and remain in a non-threatening pose. Ideally, don't stand up over a small animal on ground level or have your hands up and palms facing out like a predator about to pounce.

Respect a few golden rules: give animals the power of choice; always respect boundaries; let go of expectations.

Initially stay 5-10 feet away from the animal. Allow the animal to come to you if they wish, and if not, remember you will be just as effective from a short distance! It is more important that the animal has choice than that you have your hands on them! Once they realize that they can choose whether to receive Reiki, and that you will let them choose how to receive the treatment, many animals will come up and place different body parts on your hands, depending on what their healing needs are, and their comfort level with the energy. By not forcing hands-on treatment, you are building trust and confidence, allowing the animal to be an active participant in the healing process.

Let go of your expectations about how an animal should behave during the treatment (they usually do not behave like humans, lying down motionless for 60 minutes). The typical treatment consists of an ebb and flow of hands-on/short distance Reiki as well as short periods of movement and relaxation. Also, let go of your expectations about what healing result the animal should manifest.

Hand positions are not important.

Animal treatment is very different than human treatment: You may be drawn to certain areas, or the animal may want you to focus on certain areas. You may do only one or two positions during the whole treatment. Remember, Reiki will go where it needs to go, regardless of where your hands are, so focus on what the animal wants and let him or her show you the best positions (if any) to use!

Do not force a treatment.

Signs of Acceptance: eye contact, pushing body into your hands, lying down or falling asleep, sighs, deep breaths, yawns; also you may feel the flow of energy in your hands or other parts of your body.

Signs that an animal is saying "no" to treatment: They will move as far away as possible, turn away, avoid eye contact AND remain agitated for more than a few minutes. The main sign is they will not settle or relax after several minutes.

Intuition during the treatment.

Physical or emotional information may be received during a treatment. Often practitioner may need to do nothing with this info, but sometimes it may help move things along to share with the animal's person. Always do so with discretion and compassion.

- *Physical insights*: aches/pains/cold/heat in hands, arms or other parts of the body. Stay there (either in person or on surrogate) until it subsides (indicates need for more Reiki).

- *Emotional Information*: visual images, thoughts or feelings: These can be strong and disconcerting but will go away, and are not "yours".

Enhancing Intuition

Over time, intuition will deepen with regular practice. Anything the animal chooses to share with you is a sign of trust and a great honor; you being the witness can help them begin to release these feelings/memories and move on.

**Remember, it is NOT necessary to receive intuitive information in order for the treatment to be effective: remember, it is Reiki, NOT YOU that is doing the healing! For many people, however, enhanced and deepened intuition is a wonderful "side-effect" of giving Reiki.

What is a healing reaction?

Definition: Issues deeply buried and hidden come to the surface to release as they heal. When this happens, the body may respond to healing by appearing to get worse (physically or emotionally). Usually these are only brief symptoms and are accompanied by signs of recovery. Subsequent Reiki treatments can help ease reactions. It's good to remind yourself, if you observe an animal having a healing reaction, that Reiki can do no harm: anything that comes up is for the good of the being. And one more gentle reminder: as part of the healing space, you yourself may experience some clearing in the form of a reaction; you also may find animals coming into your life who bring your own healing challenges to the surface.

Ending a Treatment

It is always nice to create a little ritual to bring yourself back when finishing a Reiki treatment. For example, you might place your hands over your heart or in gassho (palms together in front of your heart) and say "Thank you Reiki" three times (this reminds you that you are merely a channel for the energy). It is also good to thank the animal for his participation and acceptance. Remember to trust Reiki and accept the outcome of the treatment, whatever it may be.

Frequency and Duration of Treatments

- Always start with a series of four treatments if possible. The strength of treatments support each other when given close together.

- Serious or chronic conditions benefit from once or more treatments per week.

- Small problems benefit from once a week until problem resolves.

- Surgery: Once a day 3-5 days preceding surgery, and once a day for about a week afterwards.

- Dying animals benefit from one or more small treatments per day.

- EVERY animal benefits from regular treatments (once a week or every other week) for energetic balance and health maintenance.

Treating Animals and People Together

Sometimes, even though it may be the animal who is sick, the person also needs healing: healing from stress, healing from fear and worry, healing from grief. For this reason, it is often preferable to offer Reiki to the animal AND the person at the same time. There are two ways to do this:

1)   Offering a chair treatment to the person and inviting the animal into the space.

     Offer the animal's person a chair treatment and invite the animal to be in the room during the treatment. Signs that an animal is participating in the treatment are signs of relaxation or sleep. Some movement of the animal during treatment is common; just relax and open your intention that you are holding this beautiful space of peace and healing for all.

2)   Offering a treatment to an animal and inviting the person to share the meditation.

     Lead the person in a meditation and ask them to sit and observe during the rest of the treatment. Set your intention to hold a beautiful space of peace and healing for all. The animal will appreciate that their person is in the room with you, and the quiet time with all of you together is very healing.

Distant Healing for Animals

When we use the term "distant healing", we are referring to the practice of offering Reiki outside of the animal's physical presence. Remember, however, that physical distance is only a surface human perception. By focusing inward to that very deepest spiritual core of ourselves (and the symbols and mantras are tools to help us do this), we can remember, realize and experience that in reality we are all connected and all One—in other words, distance is only one plane of existence—one that is most easily perceived by our human senses in our physical bodies. In offering "distant healing," in reality, we are not so much offering "distant" Reiki as just accessing our innate connection to each other, our "Oneness," and offering Reiki in that connected space.

Distant Healing is very effective and can be preferable to in-person treatments in some instances. Some animals may be extremely small, fearful of strangers, wild or feral, old and fragile or close to death and may be better able to relax and absorb Reiki outside of the practitioner's physical presence. For shelter and sanctuary volunteers with very busy schedules, alternating distant and in-person Reiki treatments are a great way to be able to support the animals with Reiki more often. Distant healing is also quick to schedule: in emergency situations, we can usually offer distant healing within a day (sometimes even immediately!) of being contacted. Similarly, if an animal seems to be coming down with something or needs additional support between in-person visits, distant healing will provide needed support.

Distant Reiki offers the same benefits as in-person Reiki; it supports the animal's self-healing on physical, emotional, and spiritual levels. For example, distant healing can help with pain relief for various illnesses and injuries, accelerated healing from surgery, emotional healing, including healing for behavioral issues, prevention of illness or accelerated healing of an illness, and can create a peaceful space for the transition to death.

Tips for Distant Healing:

- When doing distant healing, your intention to heal is more important than the form and exact wording you may use.

- Visualize or use a photo of the person, animal, or situation to whom you want to send distant healing.

- Healing can be sent to the past, present, or future in the same way.

- Hold hands up or in lap and mentally offer the Reiki to the being or situation.

- Cup hands together, shrink the being or situation in your mind to fit inside your hands.

- Place hands over a photo, stuffed animal, or doll that represents the being you want to treat.

- Any object can be used to represent the body of the being you intend to treat. This object/surrogate simply helps your focus.

- For multiple treatments, write on paper the being's name or description, or a short description of the situation that needs healing and place it into a box. You can then hold the box or think about the box as you offer Reiki.

- At the end of the treatment, set your intention to finish, and gassho in thanks.

- Distant healing usually ranges from around 20 to 45 minutes in length. Just as in regular Reiki treatments, the practitioner should follow her intuition about when the treatment "feels" finished. For example, when the flow of energy dissipates, or when the practitioner comes out of her meditative state, or if in the presence of the animal, when the animal comes out of his relaxed state.

Suggested Topics for Introducing People to Animal Reiki

What Is Reiki?

The word "Reiki" means, literally, "spiritual energy." It refers to the energy that makes up all things in the universe—in other words, the energetic substance that quantum physicists talk about and study. Reiki "the system," on the other hand, refers to a Japanese system created by Mikao Usui in the late 19th and early 20th centuries. The original purpose of the system was spiritual development, but in modern times the emphasis has evolved as a system of energetic healing, utilizing specific Japanese meditative practices and breathing techniques. Reiki for humans is successfully utilized as a supportive healing technique in medical settings such as hospitals, cancer centers, hospice programs and AIDS clinics all over the country. Reiki is lesser known as a holistic system for animals, but as knowledge of human Reiki's successes and benefits spreads, more and more human companions are seeking out Reiki as a healing support for their beloved animals.

What Does a Reiki Practitioner Do?

Reiki practitioners use intention, focus and meditation to build a sort of energetic "healing bridge." The bridge is built upon the foundation of the practitioner's dedication to his or her Reiki personal practice, energetic experience and purity of intention. The bridge itself consists of the energetic harmony and balance that is the essence of Reiki. When animals are stressed, sick or injured, you could say that, energetically, they are "imbalanced." By offering an energetic connection and bridge of "balance," the practitioner is offering the animal a support system that the animal can use to relax, self-heal and "rebalance."

What Does a Reiki Practitioner *Not* Do?

Reiki sessions are given for the purpose of stress reduction and relaxation to promote healing. Reiki is not a substitute for medical diagnosis and treatment. Reiki practitioners do not diagnose conditions nor do they prescribe, perform medical treatment nor interfere with the treatment of a licensed medical professional. Reiki practitioners do not manipulate energy or control treatments; animals are the leaders in the process, taking only the amount of energy they wish to receive.

How Can Reiki Help Animals?

In the energetic space of healing, all possibilities exist, and common healing effects are signs of peace, well-being and relaxation during treatment that lead to physical, emotional and/or spiritual improvement and healing.

Reiki Can:

- Maintain health and well-being on the physical, mental and emotional levels.
- Induce deep relaxation and stress-relief.
- Accelerate healing in sick or injured animals, or animals recovering from surgery.
- Help reduce pain and inflammation.
- Help reduce behavior problems and aggression.
- Help abused animals heal from past mental/physical trauma.

- Complement conventional and alternative therapies.
- Lessen the side effects of other medical treatments.
- Support the dying process.

Why Is Reiki an Ideal Holistic Therapy for Animals?

- It is gentle, noninvasive, painless and stress-free.
- It goes to the issues that need it most, even when unknown to the practitioner.
- It can be given hands-on or from a distance and adapted to any problem an animal may face.
- It can do no harm to either recipient or practitioner.
- Animals can control their participation in the treatment, thus becoming leaders in their own process of healing.

What Creates a Successful Reiki Treatment?

A successful animal Reiki treatment requires just two things: the intention of the practitioner to be an open channel for the energy, and the acceptance the animal gives to this energy.

What Does a Typical Treatment Look Like?

Every treatment is different, as every animal will choose to receive Reiki in his or her own way; however, there are two main signs that an animal is accepting the treatment:

1) Signs of relaxation (yawning, deep relaxed breathing, sleeping and so on)

2) Ebb and flow movement: The animal may come to and fro from your hands, walk away then come back, lay down to rest then get up and so on. This pattern may be repeated many times within the course of one 30-minute session.

Rarely, an animal may choose to reject a Reiki treatment. Behavior such as annoyance, aggravation and/or nervousness will be displayed, along with an inability to settle.

Is Reiki for Animals a "Hands-on" Healing System?

Although a human Reiki treatment usually consists of a series of hand positions lightly placed upon different parts of the body, an animal Reiki treatment is approached very differently. When doing Reiki on an animal, it is best to treat from several feet away and allow the animal to come forward to receive hands-on treatment only if he or she is open to it. Many animals will actually place certain body parts into the hands of the practitioner to show where they need healing the most. Other animals will simply lie down several feet away and fall into a deep "Reiki nap." Because animal Reiki treatments are not dependent upon physical contact for success, they are ideal for use with shelter animals. Animals who are fearful, skittish, abused or aggressive are ideal candidates for Reiki from a distance. Practitioners can offer Reiki quite successfully whether physical contact is used or not.

CHAPTER NINE

INTRODUCTION TO THE HARA SYSTEM

The Three Diamonds

In the Japanese tradition, there are three energetic centers, "the three diamonds". The most well-known is the Hara, which literally means stomach, abdomen or belly. Energy is stored at this point of the body and from there it expands throughout the whole body. The other two centers are located at the head and the center of the chest. By clearing and connecting all three energy centers, the practitioner creates unity and balance.

This energetic system is the backbone of the system of Reiki.

As taught by the the International House of Reiki, these three diamonds correspond to the energy of Earth (Jap: chi), Heaven (Jap: ten) and Oneness or Humanity (Jap: jin). The Earth center is located just below the navel at the Hara, the Heavenly center is located in the head and the Oneness center is located in the Heart (middle of the chest).

In traditional Japanese teachings and exercises that are still practiced today, this energetic system remains the main focus for building a person's energy.

> *Always try to remain in communion with Heaven and Earth; then the universe will appear in its true light. If you perceive the true form of Heaven and Earth, you will be enlightened to your own true self.* -Quote from Morihei Ueshiba, founder of Aikido

The Three Diamonds Meditation
(as taught by the International House of Reiki)

The following technique is wonderful to use on your own as self-healing or with another person. When offering to a person, it's easiest to do when both practitioner and receiver are in the standing position. It's also a great practice to do in the presence of animals! To share this technique with animals, simply set your intent at the beginning that you "invite the animals also to share this beautiful space for healing."

1) Place both your hands palm over palm an inch apart and a few inches off the body over the Hara. Feel the connection.

2) Move both your hands to the center of the chest (heart), palm over palm and an inch apart, a few inches off the body and stay until you once again begin to feel a connection. Imagine that you have connected the Hara with the heart center.

3) Now move your hands to the forehead, palm over palm an inch apart and just off the body and again stay until you feel the connection. Imagine that you have connected the heart with the mind.

4) Bring your hands to the heart center again, feel that connection. Then bring your hands to your Hara center again and so on. Repeat this pattern at your own pace for 20-30 minutes. Make sure to finish at the Hara.

Developing the earth and sky together within our bodies through the practices of Reiki brings peace, equanimity, balance and perfect, lasting healing—beyond the physical body; it is the healing of our eternal spirit. This peacefulness is always there, no matter what struggles we or our animals will face. Grounding in the earth and letting ourselves expand into the sky allows us to remember our true natures. Our Reiki practice gives us the tools to uncover our inner bright light that is always perfect and beautiful, no matter what struggles we, or our animals, may face on the surface.

In the following chapters, we will discuss the benefits of developing our hara, and explore meditations which center around them.

CHAPTER TEN

GROUNDING

All About Grounding

Grounding makes us think of the earth, but in reality it is being present in the moment. This presence creates strength and allows us to find our balance.

The animals will keep you grounded! They do this by helping us to become more present in the moment in our bodies. And meditation will further nurture that mindful, present state so that we can bring this balance more fully into our lives.

Why is it so hard to ground?

There are many reasons; here are just a few:

- Civilization is so separated from nature
- Our lives are usually indoors rather than out
- We no longer pay attention to the rhythms of nature
- We are too busy and always multitasking
- Most of our activities are intellect based; therefore we are always in our heads. This is upside-down from where we should be.

What are the things that work against grounding?

Our culture nurtures drama "emotional highs and lows." We see this on reality shows and popular TV shows, magazines, internet news sites (I call it the "bad news") and videos that manipulate our emotions. All of this media feeds emotions like fear and upset or anger. In essence when we watch these shows/read these stories day after day we are practicing imbalance; we are nurturing all the qualities that take away from our harmony and ability to stay strong in difficult situations.

Why is grounding so important when working with Reiki and our animals?

When our animals sense that we are carried away with emotion, our energy feels very out of balance, and this might make it difficult for them to connect to us. If they themselves are facing something difficult such as a physical or emotional hurdle or struggle, if we mirror their anxiety, their sadness, etc., we are only adding to their difficulties. On the other hand, if we are grounded, our animals can come to us no matter what their issues, and they will feel a nurturing, harmonious space that doesn't change in us. This will help them to trust us and search us out when they need support!

When we are grounded, we are in balance. When we are grounded and balanced, we are empowered, because we are conscious. With consciousness comes choice. We are empowered to choose peace over anger, courage over fear, joy over sadness and so on. When we are balanced we may be of service to others. This service is our highest calling in this life.

How can we develop our grounding?

We can only become more grounded by gathering the energy which we normally find scattered everywhere. The more we learn to gather this dissipated energy, the more present in the moment we become. A great way to gather our energy is through regular practice of meditations that nurture our inner earth energy, Physically, we will find our grounding center at the hara below the navel. In the following chapter we will explore meditations that can help us to ground.

CHAPTER ELEVEN

GROUNDING MEDITATIONS

Mini-Meditation – Grounding

Sit or stand near your animal. Breathe in through your nose filling your entire body with beautiful healing light, all the way to your lower belly. Breathe out and expand this light out of your body and into the universe. Repeat 10 times. Invite your animal into this peaceful space.

The Healing Tree and Power Animal Meditation

Find a comfortable position to sit or stand near your animal. Relax your shoulders and arms. Relax your body and legs. Close your eyes or keep them open in soft focus and take a couple of deep breaths into your belly.

Imagine that you are a beautiful strong tree. Your roots stretch deep into the earth and your branches reach high into the sky. Next to you, in the lovely shade of your branches, lays a large and powerful tiger. She leans against your trunk, her large paws stretched out and relaxed. She is at once stunning, powerful and strong, and yet at this moment she is simply quiet and thoughtful, fully present with you, as a tree. You can feel her fierceness, courage and the fiery energy of her vibrant heart— this is an ancient energy deeply connected to the earth and full of wisdom and compassion.

She is here to share her power so that you can remember how to access your inner strength from a stable and grounded place. She will help you remember that in this moment, all healing possibility exists within you, and this will help you have the courage to face whatever healing issues you or your loved ones may face. Say yes to this sharing of energy with the tiger, yes to remembering your inner courage, yes to healing potential and possibility. Take a moment to feel your connection to her, no separation. All one.

With the assistance of the tiger beside you, imagine the ancient wisdom of earth can flow up your roots grounding and stabilizing you. Imagine your branches reach out of your crown and up into the limitless universe. Feel warm healing light of compassion shining down on all your branches—this is the expansive energy of sky. Compassion can move down your branches, into your crown and through your trunk. Feel ancient wisdom moving up from the earth, and expansive compassion shining down from the sky, mixing within your tree.

Feel the tiger supporting you to deeply experience this wisdom and compassion, which creates a deep and strong courage within you. You are strong, stable, grounded. You can feel courage within you creating a beautiful bright light that spreads out from your tree, expanding the healing gifts of wisdom and compassion out into the world around you.

Now I'd like you to bring to your mind an animal in your life who is facing illness. See him or her sitting under your tree, next to your healing tiger of courage. Very gently invite him/her to share in the limitless healing power of ancient wisdom and expansive compassion: the gifts of the earth and the sky and the tiger. Invite him/her to sit beneath your healing branches. Feel the light of your tree and tiger shining so brightly that all healing potential exists in this very moment. Healing for body, mind and spirit is possible *now*. Feel the tiger helping you access inner courage to be able to hold this healing space for your special animal, no matter what issues are faced. Feel peace radiate from your tree, from your tiger, and also now from your special animal who has joined you in this space.

Relax into this peaceful healing energy. Feel that within this space is simply a state of being—nothing to do, nothing to fix, no worries or fear. Within this space you can simply surrender to the flow of the universe. Within this space, the universe understands healing and balance at the ultimate levels. Feel how easy this letting go can happen with the support of your tree and your tiger. Let go and simply be.

For several minutes, in your mind, recite these words: Peaceful Mind. Peaceful Heart. Peaceful Body. Healed Mind. Healed Heart. Healed Body.

Now take a moment to thank your special animal for his/her openness to the healing. Thank your tree for helping you access your grounding and expansiveness. Thank your tiger for reminding you of your inner strength and courage. Remember that your inner tiger and inner tree of healing wisdom and compassion is always there inside of you, whenever you need it.

When you are ready, take a nice deep cleansing breath, and slowly come back and open your eyes.

Be The Mountain Meditation

Sit indoors or stand outside near your animal in a comfortable position, spine straight, shoulders and arms relaxed. Eyes remain open and in soft-focus. Relax and set your intent to experience yourself as a mountain. Tall. Broad. Ageless.

See yourself covered in grasses and trees, rocks and streams and waterfalls. There are many animals of all kinds that live in a beautiful balanced ecosystem upon your mountain. There are also people who have built their tiny fragile structures upon your mountainsides.

You can see so deeply into the nature of things. You see that your rocks and rivers mirror the veins and organs of the animals and other creatures, and of the leaves, trunk and roots of the trees. You can see so clearly that we are not so different from one another.

You hold all of these plants and creatures effortlessly.

Time passes. Feel the sun rising and setting, watch the moon cross the sky above you, see the seasons changing, storms and rain coming and going. The years quietly pass.

As the years flow by, you see the lives of the beings upon you are short and fleeting, yet beautiful. The trees live much longer than the animals and yet they too will come and go with time, with weather, or sometimes with a natural fire or lightning.

As the mountain you hold all of this without judgment, without worry, without resistance to change. You hold it with peace, with surrender and with compassion.

You will feed the plants with your soil; you will water all beings with your rivers. You will nurture all life and all beings. You will do this from a space of perfect balance and harmony.

Now within this beautiful peaceful space, I'd like you to imagine an animal or person you want to connect to for healing. See them sitting with you now. You are the mountain.

Very gently and simply, invite them into your space of strength, peacefulness, harmony and balance. It is very easy to connect with them from a space of peace. Relax into this feeling of strength and connection for several minutes.

Take a moment to thank them for their openness to connecting. Now see all the elements of you as the mountain again: nurturing, compassionate, strong, balanced. Remember you always have access to these qualities within you; you just have to remember them.

When you are ready, take a nice deep cleansing breath and come back and open your eyes.

Being Peace With Your Animal Meditation

Sit indoors or stand outside near your animal in a comfortable position, spine straight, shoulders and arms relaxed. Eyes remain open and in soft-focus. Place your hands over your lower belly. Relax your entire body as you breathe deeply a few times.

Imagine there are roots growing down from the base of your spine, deep and wide into the earth. Imagine that the powerful, grounding energy of the earth can flow up these roots into your lower belly giving you stability and peace.

Take ten breaths, and on each inhale, feel peaceful earth energy coming up into your lower belly. On each exhale, release any emotions, fears or worries you may have out your roots, easily dissolving them into the peacefulness that is earth. The earth is so strong that it can easily dissipate these fears and worries into perfect pure light that nourishes. With each successive breath, feel more and more stillness and stability within you. Once you have completed the ten breaths, allow yourself to relax in the space of earth energy and stability that you have created with your breath.

Once you feel yourself fully calm and connected to the earth, simply invite your animal into the peaceful space you have created with your breath. Imagine that within this space, all is perfect and balanced and that your animal can join you. Feel harmony enveloping both you and your animal. Let go of your expectations (along with any worries about what needs to be healed) and continue to breathe the calm and strength of earth energy into your belly as you share this space with your animal.

Place your hands gently on your animal if he approaches, or keep them on your belly if he chooses to remain at a distance. Signs of relaxation and stress-relief in your animal will indicate that he is sharing your peaceful healing space with you.

Meditation for Going to the Veterinarian

Practice this meditation five minutes a day, twice a day for a few days leading up to your vet visit if possible. If not, try it at home before you leave. While you are on your way, and even after you arrive at the vet, continue the breath and revisit the positive images as much as possible.

Sit or stand in a comfortable position and place your hands over your lower belly (this is your energetic foundation, your connection to the earth, your grounding and center). Close your eyes or keep them open in soft focus and breathe. As you breathe in, imagine light is flowing up from the earth through your feet and the base of your spine into your lower belly. On the out breath, imagine this light can move up into the rest of your body, until your entire body is filled with a beautiful, glowing light. Breathe deeply and slowly. Feel the strength and calm of your breath stabilizing you and the light dissolving any worries or concerns. When you feel centered, visualize the upcoming car ride to the vet, the walk into the office, and being with the veterinarian with your dog. Picture in your mind your dog getting treats if the vet gives them out (or bring your own to reward your doggie for his bravery while you are there!). As you continue to breathe in earth energy, it's important to stay positive in your thoughts. Visualize the vet as friendly, helpful, trustworthy—as you and your dog's ally and friend. See your dog's behavior and emotional state as calm, helpful and brave. See yourself as a stable and confident partner, supporting your dog during the visit. Imagine how effortless and easy this visit will be, and that you will be home soon after.

Being Courage Meditation

Sit in a comfortable position in a room near your animal (no physical contact is needed), spine straight, shoulders and arms relaxed. Relax your entire body as you breathe deeply a few times.

Imagine there are roots growing down from the base of your spine, deep and wide into the earth. Imagine that the powerful, grounding energy of the earth can flow up these roots into your heart center, giving you stability and peace. Take 10 breaths, and on each in-breath, feel the earth energy coming up into your heart. On each out-breath, release any emotions, fears or worries you may feel inside you. With each successive breath, feel more and more stillness and stability within you.

Once you have completed the 10 breaths, allow yourself to sit for several minutes in the space of earth energy and stability that you have created with your breath. Once you feel yourself fully calm and connected to the earth, bring your animal to your mind. Imagine that your heart can expand out of your body, creating a beautiful state of courage and trust all around you. Call upon any memories or experiences that may help you to truly *feel* courage and deep trust within your body, mind and spirit.

Once you feel a strong sense of *being* courage, simply invite your animal into the space. Imagine that within this heart space, all is harmonious and balanced. Feel a strong bond of trust connecting you to your animal. Let go of your expectations (along with any worries about what needs to be healed) and continue to breathe the courage and calm of earth energy into your heart as you share this space with your animal.

Earth Practice Meditation

Find a place to sit directly on the earth. Alternately, place a chair on the earth so that at least your feet can be flat on the ground. Place your hands over your lower belly (Hara). As you inhale, imagine the breath as light flowing up from the earth, into your legs, body and into your belly. As you exhale, feel the breath flowing from your lower belly, down your legs and feet and returning to the earth. Imagine this light can connect you to the core of the earth: with each breath it can travel instantaneously from your Hara to core of the earth and back again. With each breath, imagine the light grows brighter and brighter, both at your Hara and in the core of the earth, the energy circulating back and forth. Feel your lower body becoming heavier and heavier, as if there is no separation between you and the earth's center.

After several minutes focusing on your breath, relax and just sit in the energy. Feel the energy in your Hara as bright, warm light. Just as your hands are connected to the Hara, all of your being is connected to your Hara. Feel as if your Hara is no different from the core of the earth. The same beautiful light emanates from your Hara and the earth's core. Feel the stability and strength of the earth within your own center.

Imagine this light can expand, filling your whole body with a beautiful bright light. Your inner light is the light of the earth—feel every cell of your body radiating the stability of earth. You are a mountain, even more, you are all mountains, and in fact you are the very planet.

Bring your awareness to the present moment. Feel the strength of earth ripple out your body, into your emotions and into your spirit, making you stronger and stronger, just as the energy of earth ripples out into space. The earth moves in space yet is stable and balanced within the universe. Your life changes unexpectedly, yet you are stable like a mountain; you are as balanced and strong as the earth itself.

Do the earth practice for yourself for several minutes until you feel your mind and body relax into the energy. Then simply invite the animal into the space for whatever they might need. Don't try to "do" anything, or push the energy towards the animal. Just imagine that you *are* the earth and you are there, strong and stable, for the animal in this present moment. You are there for whatever this moment looks like, for whatever they might need. Let go of the need to "do" and "fix." Just be. Share the space of strength, balance and harmony.

The Ocean Meditation

Go to the ocean for a few hours. Sit in the sand near the water, make yourself comfortable and just *be* with the waves. Tune into your five senses:

- What does the ocean look like? See its movement, shapes, and colors.

- How does it sound? Listen to it crashing and splashing.

- What does it smell like? Allow yourself to breathe in the ocean scent deeply and slowly.

- How might it taste?

- How would it feel to be in the waves?

Let your memories and senses run wild for a time. After a while you will notice that your thoughts lessen, and you begin to relax and feel the ocean on a deeper level. Time may seem to stand still, and you may feel as if you can stay where you are indefinitely, you are so relaxed and at peace. Notice the ebbs and flows of the wave sets as they come in and out. Notice the tide as it moves up or down the beach. Let the comforting sound, movement, and repetition of the waves carry you away, mentally and spiritually.

Begin to feel your connection with the ocean—how the movement inside your own body (pulse, heartbeat, blood circulation, breathing) might echo the movement of the ocean. Notice the stillness that resides deep within the strong motion that is the ocean.

The Tree Meditation

Find a big, strong healthy tree in your yard or local area that you can visit quietly, without being disturbed. Set your intention that you are open to receive wisdom and healing through connecting with this tree.

With your feet about shoulder's width apart, stand close to the tree and place your hands lightly on the trunk. Breathe in and out, with your eyes open in soft focus. Allow your senses to open to all the sounds and smells around you. Imagine the roots of the tree beneath you. Feel the solidity and strength of the tree trunk beneath your hands. Smell the aroma of the tree. See the patterns of the bark and the design of the branches stretching up into the sky above you. Listen to the leaves as they blow in the breeze.

Imagine you can breathe in the earth energy beneath you, up through the soles of your feet, and breathe out the crown of your head into the expansiveness of the sky above. Imagine your feet are the trees' roots, your body is the trees' trunk and your head and arms are the trees' branches. Feel yourself connecting to the energy of the tree, and more than that, becoming one with it. How does it feel to be this tree? Notice the energetic movement that resides deep within the stillness that is the tree. Just stand and *be* with the tree in this energy of earth and sky.

Healing Rock Meditation

Sit or stand comfortably with your animal. Close your eyes, or keep them open with a soft focus. Set your intention to share a grounded space with your animal. Imagine you are a giant rock on the side of a craggy mountain, high up in the clouds. Place your hands so that they are palms down on your lap.

As you breathe in, imagine the breath moves from the earth, up your feet, spine, and hands, filling your whole body. On the out breath, imagine the breath returning down your body and back into the earth. In time this breath will have a circular feeling to it, curving up from the earth and through your body and back into the earth and so on. With each breath, feel your strength, stability, and connection to the earth growing stronger. Your body begins to feel heavier and heavier. At the same time, your emotions begin to feel lighter and lighter. It is as if the closer you come to earth, the more peaceful your mind can become.

Once you have created this peaceful, rooted place within yourself, imagine that you can hold that space for your animal. Simply "invite" him into the space of your rock for healing. Within this space, there is perfect balance and calm, no matter what struggles are faced. Hold this space for as long as you like, revisiting the in and out breaths when needed for focus.

Healing Water Meditation

Sit or stand comfortably near your animal and close your eyes, or keep them open with a soft focus. Imagine you are sitting in a Japanese garden next to a koi pond. Many beautiful and colorful koi reside just below the surface of the water near to you. Set your intention to connect with these koi. Feel what it would be like to live so closely to the element of water. Imagine you can submerge yourself like a koi in the water, and with each in-breath, visualize water energy flowing through your whole being. On each out-breath, expand this water energy out into the universe around you. Feel the strength of the water filling your entire being and helping your energy expand outward in courage.

The water shows us how to be with our animals: gentle and still when we need to be, yet strong and flexible, too. Feel how connecting to the koi helps you to experience what it is to *be* water. Feel your whole being showered with a peaceful strength. Feel water washing away fears and uncertainties and purifying and strengthening your energy. Invite your animal to share this peaceful, strong space with you. Relax your breath, and just sit together with your animal in this beautiful water element for as long as you like. Within this space you have all the courage you need to face whatever difficulties lay before you.

Meditation with the Hara, the Precepts and Animals

Sit comfortably with your palms resting on your lap. Now close your eyes and take a nice deep cleansing breath, and let it out slowly. We will do some Hara breathing to help get us centered.

I'd like you to breathe in through your nose, filling your body with beautiful healing light all the way down to the Hara, which is your lower belly, below your belly button. And on the out breath, I'd like you to imagine that this light can expand out your skin, out into your aura, and out into the universe. Continue to breathe in through your nose, filling your body with healing light and connecting to the Hara. Continue to breathe out, expanding this light out into the universe.

Continue this Hara breathing for a few minutes. With each breath in, feel your connection to the Hara growing stronger and deeper, and with each breath out, feel yourself expanding wider and wider into the universe. Breathe in, connecting to the Hara. Breathe out, expanding into the universe.

Return your breath to normal and take a minute; just sit in that beautiful space of energy created with your breath. Energy is inside of you, and all around you. Feel the easy flow, the balance and peace.

Just for today, do not anger. Do not worry. Be humble. Be honest in your work. Be compassionate to yourself and to others. Simply reflect upon these five precepts.

Now I'd like you to bring to mind an animal in your life. I'd like you to bring together the precepts and this animal, reflecting on the ways that your animal embodies the values of the precepts or perhaps the way this animal helps you to embody those precepts more fully in your life.

For today, do not anger. Do not worry. Be humble. Be honest in your work. Be compassionate to yourself and to others. I'd like you to open your heart to your animal teacher and realize that they are always there either to show you how to embody these precepts or to inspire you to embody them within yourself. In this way, they are very deep spiritual teachers.

Open your heart to listening and to being present. Realize that you can receive the wisdom of the precepts with the help of your animal. When we go deeper into the teachings of the precepts, then they can ripple out more fully into our lives.

In this way, your animals will support you in letting go of anger, letting go of worry, living with humility, honesty, and compassion.

Your animals can help you to transform your life and live within the precepts. Our life is healing and healing is our life.

Take a moment to thank your animal or animals for sharing this space today. Whoever appeared within the meditation was just perfect; feel gratitude, and also remember to keep your heart open so that you can hear these lessons from your animals.

When you're ready, you can set your intention to finish. Take a nice deep cleansing breath and slowly come back and open your eyes.

CHAPTER TWELVE

EXPANSION

All About Expansion

Meditation helps us to uncover the spacious, expanded nature of our relaxed consciousness. This happens when we let go of our thoughts and intellectual mind and just sit in the perfect stillness of the Reiki space. So many times in our lives we are focusing on regrets in the past, worries about the future, or trying to control the present moment—our minds are so busy "doing" that we forget about "being!"

But what if this present moment is difficult? When going through a challenge such as a life-threatening illness, we might find our thoughts slowly getting more and more focused on the problem. Dwelling on our animal's physical suffering, worrying about the pain and side-effects of treatments and surgeries, fears about if/when they will recover—these kinds of thoughts become like thick clouds covering the vast nature of our minds. Sometimes it might feel like they *are* the disease, and that there is nothing but pain, fear or a bad ending. In this way, our minds become smaller and more boxed in, darker and more depressed. Focusing on the negative causes us to forget our expansiveness.

When we expand the mind, we can see our animal's true essence.

In reality, no matter what is "wrong" with our animals, their inner essence is eternal, is bright, is beautiful, is perfect, is connected to all things and is as wide as the universe. Our animal's true essence is always free and always well. Sharing Reiki with our animals helps us to connect with this spiritual part, no matter what our animals are going through physically. Maybe the pain is still there, maybe we still have some fear about outcomes, but Reiki helps take away the overwhelming nature of things. Reiki helps us realize there is *more*. With Reiki, we can sense and feel so much more possibility—compassion as wide as the universe, healing potential as deep as forever. This recognition of the larger spiritual self can offer relief and comfort from suffering for both our animals and us.

Allowing our minds to expand helps the animals. Over the years, I have had many amazing Reiki experiences with shelter animals. These were animals who were frightened, abused or traumatized. Some of them were suffering terrible injuries or illnesses, even dying, yet when I would sit with them in the Reiki space, and allow my mind to let go—completely let go of worries, fears, judgments, expectations, all of it—then, as I felt my mind relax, I would see that even the animals with the most suffering would be able to lie down peacefully, take a deep sigh, and truly relax. The reality of being in a shelter hadn't changed, their health hadn't changed (often healing or adoption miracles do shortly follow treatments!) and yet they were able to find peace and wellbeing even in the midst of that difficult situation. What a miracle!

We can help to relieve suffering through expansive consciousness.

Although we often see that Reiki lessens pain and improves physical or mental issues, it's not always that Reiki necessarily removes the suffering, but it just puts it in perspective. Suffering might be there, yes, but it's not the only thing that is there; it's not the only thing that we are. I suppose we could say that suffering is part of life, but the question is, do we let ourselves be overwhelmed by it? If we can stay grounded and stable, while also finding a way to touch our expansive consciousness, suffering loses its strong grip and we can find our way back to balance.

For me that's the real gift of Reiki—not that it will prevent anything bad from ever happening to us—there are always bumps in the road of life—however Reiki can help us to stay in touch with our true nature, which always and at every moment, no matter what we are facing, has the capacity to experience peace, harmony and relief from suffering.

Reiki with animals is not an outward activity of "doing"… rather it is an inward mental state of being… an inner intention to peel back our own layers to find our true nature, the nature that is expansive and infinite. In accessing this reality of connectedness with the universe, we also access infinite healing potential and possibility.

Recently in a Reiki class I was teaching at a farm sanctuary, I took the students into the sheep paddock. Their assignment was to choose a spot away from the sheep (the sheep all ran for cover when they saw us coming, disappearing into the barn) and meditate: focusing on their breathing—relaxing into a peaceful space within themselves. Without expectation and judgments, this mental space becomes very expansive.

It took a few moments for every student to find a spot and settle into their meditation, but after about ten minutes, the sheep began slowly peeking their curly little heads out the door of the barn. Then slowly they began to venture into the yard, one following the other in a perfect line up. The students remained motionless, many of them with eyes closed, focusing inward, rather than outward on the progress of the sheep. Slowly the sheep's courage built and several of them began to move forward to make physical contact with some of the students. A few other sheep chose spots in the yard near students to lie down for a Reiki nap. Others chose to stay in the barn, lying down to soak up the energy. The energy was so peaceful in the entire area; it was irresistible, even to the shy sheep! When two sheep approached me and put their heads in my hands, it was a truly humbling and amazing moment.

Keeping intuition in perspective

It's true, that Reiki deepens intuition. This means that in our treatments or meditations with animals, we may begin to feel certain sensations, or gain a deeper understanding of what the animal is feeling and going through. This is called *hibiki* or "echo" in Japanese. It is important for the Reiki practitioner to remember that the more we focus on what we are feeling and what it means – in other words, the more we interpret and judge what we receive intuitively – the more we create expectations and, in turn, worries about outcomes etc. Focusing on interpreting causes a separation between the animal and us. Reiki teachings help us to realize our innate Oneness, and in order to do this we must let go of our opinions, wishes and judgments about what is happening. Interpretations of *hibiki* can make our mind very narrow and small. The more we can let go of these thoughts, just let them float by like clouds, the more open and expanded our mind and heart can be, and the more present we can be for the animal. It is our openhearted presence, or "being" with our animals, without our judgments and interpretations, which is the real healing power of Reiki.

Expansion helps us to realize what true healing is.

Reiki is a healing system. The word "healing" is a bit of a loaded term isn't it? What exactly does healing mean? People often have certain expectations that if their animals receive a Reiki treatment all physical/emotional problems will disappear. If that were true, the world would be a very different place wouldn't it? So we have to ask ourselves, if that is not the case, what does it mean to truly heal? In reality, our bodies are finite, and we do not live forever. Does that mean that healing eventually fails us all? Or perhaps we are missing the possibility of deeper and more profound healing: the healing of our inner spirit. We can see from the Reiki precepts that Mikao Usui taught, that true and lasting healing is about our state of mind. Sometimes life is difficult and sometimes it is easy, but how do we deal with the things that come our way? Sometimes our animals will get better and sometimes it is their time to pass, but with the tools of the system of Reiki, we can create a beautiful space of peace and balance no matter what our beloved animals or we may face.

How can we expand our state of mind?

Meditation gives us the path that leads into this expansive healing potential. Relax *into* the softness and gentleness of Reiki, the healing energetic space that exists all around us, rather than trying so hard to push the energy this way and that way. Physically, this expansive potential is centered at the upper hara at the forehead. In the following chapter, we will explore several meditation practices which can help us to develop the ability to expand the mind beyond our physical eyes, to be able to truly "see" our animals.

CHAPTER THIRTEEN

EXPANSION MEDITATIONS

Opening to Possibilities

Sit or stand in a relaxed posture with your eyes closed or open in soft focus, breathing gently. Open your awareness to the "animal need" around you. Visualize yourself as you go through your day; see yourself as present, aware, and available to be a healing support in all that you do, everywhere you go, and for any animal that may choose to find you. Hold this focus for 5–10 minutes at the beginning of the day.

Awaken

Share this moment with your animal. Check in with your five senses and also your heart (emotion) to help you appreciate all details that exist right now. Tell your animal three things you are grateful for about them.

Visualize the Positives Meditation

This is a wonderful technique to use not only at the very beginning when you bring your new animal home, but also anytime you are introducing him to a new experience.

You have already prepared your home for your animal's arrival—bought a bed, leash, food and dishes, toys and treats, but don't forget to prepare your mind and emotions! Close your eyes and breathe deeply, letting all your concerns and stresses about your new arrival blow away like clouds in the sky.

Set your intent to fill your mind with positive images. Visualize lots of things about your family, and fill your heart with a feeling of joy that your animal will now also be a part of your family. You can envision joyful thoughts and emotions about your plans for including your new animal into your home and life. As your mind and emotions relax into these peaceful and joyful thoughts and emotions, you will find your new animal more than happy to connect and relax into this beautiful space with you.

Bright Light Meditation

As you share a beautiful space of connection with your animal, mentally step back from your own understanding of the things that need healing. Realize you are already filled with the light and wisdom of the healing energy of the universe. Visualize yourself shining bright with this energy that radiates from your entire being and aura. Set your intention that all your light can flow and work to support your animal in his/her healing journey, which is beyond your own conscious understanding. Allow this bright light to purify your mind of worries, concerns, and control issues. Just shine. Hold this emptiness and relaxed state of mind as the energy flows, glows and radiates.

Moonlight Beacon

Find a quiet space to meditate, where you will not be disturbed. Choose a comfortable place to sit or stand, close your eyes or keep them open in a soft focus and take a deep breath, exhaling slowly. Imagine you are sitting on the edge of a cliff, looking out to the endless sea. It is night and very dark, except for a beautiful full moon, which illuminates the surface of the waves upon the ocean.

Out there somewhere in the darkness is your animal, looking for a way back to shore. Breathe earth energy up from your roots and moon energy down through your crown. Feel your body, mind, and spirit filling with the brightest moonlight of healing and harmony. Feel your entire being becoming a beacon of balance—a moon of hope and healing for your animal.

Imagine that your animal can easily follow the bright light of healing that you radiate, and if they so choose, may navigate the dark waters to perfect safety, healing, and harmony. The path to healing is easily illuminated by the moonlight; the way becomes clear. Hold this moonlight beacon within yourself for as long as is comfortable.

Sun Illumination Meditation

Sit or stand in a comfortable position to meditate and close your eyes or keep them open in soft focus. See yourself sitting in a wide meadow in a beautiful forest. Imagine your animal is with you. The sky is cloudy and the meadow is submerged in mist, making it difficult to see. Set your intention that you are open to receive clarity in order to know the best, wisest decision to make for your animal's highest good.

Imagine that suddenly a bright ray of sunlight pierces through the mist, shining directly on you and your animal. See the clouds above you open up and the sun's rays becoming wider and stronger. Feel the sunlight warming your body and skin. Feel its light surrounding you both and expanding outward more and more.

As you breathe in, imagine the sunlight can shine even into your heart and spirit, helping you connect more deeply with your inner wisdom. See yourself and your animal, sitting in the meadow and slowly being completely (both externally and internally) engulfed in the brightest sunlight you have ever experienced. Relax for several minutes, allowing the sun to illuminate you both. Now look inside your heart. See how the sun has lit up your inner being. The answers you seek are inside you; your inner wisdom is waiting to be heard. Just take a moment to sit in the light of the sun and listen to your heart.

CHAPTER FOURTEEN

CONNECTION

All About Connection

Connecting with animals through your Reiki practice is very beneficial. Animals have a much easier time understanding that we're all connected because their senses are more highly developed. They retain their deep connection to the ancient wisdom of Mother Earth, which we have lost in our modern "civilized" society.

In addition, animals have a beautiful way of opening our hearts. There's something about them; just their presence in our lives touches us the way nothing else does. When opening our hearts to our animals, we realize there's no separation. We feel that heart connection with our animals and compassion then arises, and then we feel happy.

So this is how our animals make us happier. Of course now we have all these scientific studies about how animals help their people. For example, people who have animals have lower blood pressure, have lower rates of depression and so on. So, animals already know about healing us. But I think if we look a little more deeply, we can see it's not just that they're nice to pet and we talk to them and they're cute. It's not even just that they're there with us. It's even deeper than that. They hold a spiritual space of presence and openness, which is a living model of how we need to be living too: pure, present, without judgment and with open hearts. Reiki gives us the tools to share that space with them and connect. That beautiful space of compassion creates a space of happiness inside of us.

Transcend separateness through heart-to-heart connections

Connecting with animals during meditation is a way of connecting more deeply from our heart to the animal's heart, becoming more aware of the love and compassion that exists between us, and of our deeper connection beyond just our physical relationship. This heart connection transcends species. When we can be truly present for animals in times of health, illness, injury, or even as they go through the death and dying process, we are able to support their journey in a very profound way. We will also realize all the gifts they have given us throughout our time together. Through Reiki we also remember that no matter what happens, our animals will always be with us in our hearts.

What Reiki is really teaching us is that we are one with the universe. Thus, we should live in harmony with the flow of the universe. How does this relate to healing? When we're living in unison with our souls, with the earth, with all creatures and with the universe, it is a naturally healing space.

The universal flow we feel when we are truly connected is what our meditation practice is all about. Healing can flow more easily into our lives and into the lives of the ones that we love when we join the natural flow of the universe. The more that we let go of our ego and open our hearts, the more we can do this.

Animals are drawn to an open-hearted space.

Animals can sense when we approach them from this openhearted space, without ego, without judgment, without expectation. They know when we are truly being present with them. They will come to us and want to connect. They will support us in our meditation practice. They will support us when we need healing. They will come to us and allow us to support them when they need healing, and in that beautiful, quiet, peaceful space of meditation, they will share their wisdom with us. We will also be better able to support them. So it's a beautiful circle of healing and support.

We can see this especially with feral or wild animals or shelter animals who have been traumatized or abused. Even ones that are normally fearful will quickly gain trust.

I've seen this many times in shelters with animals who have a lot of trust issues or may have been abused and are very afraid of humans. When we go in to sit with them, with an agenda or with an ego, we go in and we say, "Well, you poor animal. You have all these problems and well, thank goodness I'm here, because I am a healer. I am here to help you poor little thing. So you just stay there and I am going to beam some healing your way."

With this approach, the very typical response from animals is to be wide-eyed, to look at us like we're crazy, and to leave as soon as possible if they're able. If not, if they're in a kennel and they're our captive audience, then we can see a lot of aggravation at our presence. They want us to leave.

Animals won't really tolerate connecting with us when we are in a space of ego. They also are very honest judges of that. If we're in that space of judgment, they won't have any part of it. In this way, they help us to see when we're not quite in the right space even if we mean well.

How can we develop our connectedness with animals?

For example, if we're going into a shelter with a lot of traumatized animals, we need to take some time before we walk into that shelter. We should take some time to ground ourselves, to connect with the earth, to open our hearts, to feel our hearts as expansive as the sky, to feel a peaceful mind and a peaceful heart within ourselves.

We can take some time to get in touch with our gratitude, for being present in this very moment. When we get in touch with that sense of connectedness, rather than the sense of "I am here to do this or that," now we are ready to walk into the shelter. Now, our energy is so different. It's so open. It's so welcoming. It's gentle. Most of all, it's so powerfully relaxing and good that the animals will love it!

Now the animals that before were afraid, aggravated, stressed or suffering, will immediately sense a change and shift when we walk in. They can't resist it. It's irresistible because it is a feeling of true connection: compassion, kindness and also joy, an inner joy that all of us can get in touch with at any time even if there is suffering.

Connection with all things means that joy and suffering go hand in hand; they are two sides of the same coin. Even though we may understand and know, for example, that a shelter animal has been through a lot, we look deeper. We see their beautiful heart, their beautiful, bright spirit shining, all that potential that is there, and this is a reflection of the very universe. This becomes easier when we practice the grounding and expansion exercises in the previous chapters. Grounding is your foundation. Expansion flows from your grounding. In the following chapter, we will explore some special meditations to put it all together and develop your middle hara: your heart.

CHAPTER FIFTEEN

CONNECTION MEDITATIONS

Connect from the Heart Meditation

Sit or stand near your animal. Make sure your spine is nice and straight and place your hands palms up on your lap, or resting gently at your sides. Close your eyes or leave them open in soft-focus, and take three deep breaths in and out. With each in-breath, imagine your breath as a beautiful white light that is coming up from the earth through the base of your spine and through your body into your heart. With each out-breath, see this white light traveling back down your body and out your spine into the earth. Feel how this breath centers you and makes you stable upon the earth. Sit in this stable space of the earth for a few moments and then visualize your heart as a beautiful orb of white light. Imagine you can expand this light out in all directions around you. With each inhale, feel the light becoming brighter and brighter at your heart, and with each exhale, see your heart's light expanding farther and farther. After a few moments focusing on your heart, just relax and let the energy of your heart flow all around you. Very gently, in your mind and with your heart, simply invite your animal into this beautiful heart space. Imagine your animal can step into or out of this space as they wish. Imagine that your two hearts can connect harmoniously. Feel peace and calm encompassing both of you. Relax and just share this connection with your animal for as long as they remain relaxed with you.

Being Gratitude Meditation

Sit or stand in a comfortable position, spine straight, with your shoulders and arms relaxed. Relax your entire body as you breathe deeply a few times.

Take 10 breaths, and on each in-breath, feel the earth energy coming up into your heart. On each out-breath, release any emotions, fears or worries you may feel inside you. With each successive breath, feel more and more stillness and stability within you. Once you have completed the 10 breaths, allow yourself to sit for several minutes in the space of earth energy and stability that you have created with your breath.

Once you feel yourself fully calm and connected to the earth, bring your animal to your mind. Allow yourself to think about the experiences you've had with your animal for which you are grateful. Focus on the parts of his or her unique being that are so special to you. Imagine that your heart can expand out of your body, creating a beautiful state of gratitude all around you. Thank you. Thank you. Simply invite your animal into the space. Imagine that within this heart space, all is perfect and balanced. Feel gratitude enveloping both you and your animal. Let go of your expectations (along with any worries about what needs to be healed) and continue to breathe the calm and strength of earth energy into your heart as you share this space of gratitude with your animal for as long as you like.

The Healing Pond Meditation (developing a gentle and open state of mind)

Symbolically, water represents strength through change, strength through remaining formless. The water on the surface of a pond may be still and peaceful, clear and pure, yet it is also very deep, and under the surface there can be so much movement of the creatures that call the pond their home. In the same way, Reiki with your animal can appear so quiet on the surface—as if you are doing nothing at all but sitting with your animal. And yet, when we look deeper, amazing healing can be happening just beneath the surface.

When we look at a pond, we can see the sky reflected in its surface—and in this way the pond can at once be grounded physical nature and reality, while at the same time it can reflect heaven and sky above—open limitless space and possibility. In this same way, when we sit with our animal in the Reiki space we can be with them, connecting in this physical moment, while also connecting to the spiritual dimension in which limitless healing possibility exists.

In one way, a pond remains the same over time, we can always count on it being there, as seasons and years pass, but in another way, every time we look at it, it may reflect something different—blue or grey skies, storm clouds, sun or rainbows. The pond will always be a mirror of this present moment in time. In this same way, we can learn to be present and open to whatever this very moment with our animal may look like—without judgment, without worry, without clinging—with love and compassion and openness.

As you sit with your animal, imagine you can pour all your light and love—your compassionate intention—into a pond. Simply invite your animal to come and drink from this healing pond for healing as they wish and as they are comfortable. Remember to relax, be patient, and remain positive. Just be in the moment with your animal. It is in this quiet, open state of mind that all healing possibilities exist...

Inner Sanctuary Meditation

Visualize a physical place in your life (a sanctuary) that brings you the most peace and calm. Let yourself imagine all the details of the place, engaging your five senses as you do. How does this place look, what colors do you see, what do you hear, and how does it smell, taste and feel? See yourself there and allow your heart and emotions to reach out and bask in the tangible peace of this sanctuary. Imagine that your very being is surrounded in healing light, just by visualizing this special place. Feel peace and calm resonating throughout your whole being. Imagine your animal can join you in this wonderful place. Invite them into the peace and calm of your sanctuary. Just relax and be in that space with your animal.

Rose of Light Meditation

Visualize your heart as a rose blooming with healing white light. Imagine this rose is composed of perfect peace, balance and harmony. Feel this light gradually spread throughout your body. After several minutes, bring to mind an animal you would like to connect with. Visualize his/her heart as a beautiful rose of healing white light. Visualize serenity and peace surrounding your animal's heart as well as yours. Imagine there is no separation; your hearts can connect together within one healing light. Visualize this unified rose of light as perfectly in balance, at peace, connected and completely healed. Hold this visualization in your mind and heart for as long as you like.

The Healing Bridge Meditation

Close your eyes and take a deep breath. Let it out slowly. Take another deep breath. Let it out slowly. Imagine that all of your stresses from the day release from you with each exhale. Breathe in. Exhale slowly. Allow yourself to let go of all your concerns and just be aware of your breath.

Now bring to your mind an animal with whom you would like to connect. See the animal here with you right now. I'd like you to imagine you can build a bridge of healing light to your animal. See this bridge extending out from your heart to the heart of your animal. This bridge represents an offering of healing light, of Reiki. It represents the possibility of healing on whatever level is needed most by your animal and a chance to find balance, peace, and harmony. Your animal has a choice now in how, or whether, to accept your offering. He or she may stay on the other side, choose to step a paw or hoof or claw or two on the bridge, meet you halfway, or perhaps walk all the way across to you.

Allow yourself to let go of your expectations about what the animal should do, and just focus on offering the healing light from your heart to your animal's heart, embracing their freedom of choice. Imagine what might happen with the bridge of light and your animal's decision.

After several minutes, thank your animal for his openness to healing possibilities, and for the lessons he has yet to teach you in healing. Slowly bring your energy bridge back to yourself. Bring all your energy back, easily and completely. Feel your energy returning to you, feel your breath returning to you. Feel yourself again bathed in the white column of light connecting you to the power of the earth and the expansiveness of the sky.

When you are ready, take a nice, deep cleansing breath and slowly come back and open your eyes, feeling refreshed and at peace.

Healing Heart, Healing Breath Meditation

Sit or stand at some distance from your animal. Feel your roots going deep into the earth and earth energy coming up your roots into your heart center. Place your hands in gassho (palms together, in front of your heart). On the in breath, bring white healing light up from the earth through the base of your spine and on up to your heart. On the out breath, expand the energy out of your heart, creating a space of light and healing all around you. Continue this in-and-out breathing pattern for several minutes. You can keep your hands in gassho or slowly open your palms and face them outward in an expansive way.

Imagine that your animal can "step in" and "step out" of the healing heart space you have created at his own discretion. Use your breath simply to hold the space and offer the possibility. After a few minutes, return your breathing to normal, rest your hands on your lap, and sit in the energy you have created for another 20-30 minutes. Watch your animal for signs of relaxation and connection with you.

Willow and Wind Meditation

Imagine you are a beautiful weeping willow tree. Your branches spread out tall and wide, reaching all the way to the ground. Your roots carry you deep into the earth, making you stable and balanced. Imagine your animal is next to you, to your weeping willow. Set your intention that you are open to facilitating healing for your animal in whatever way he is open to receive.

Imagine a wind beginning to blow. Breathe in through your roots the energy of the earth. Breathe out into the wind. Feel your breath becoming one with the wind all around you. Imagine the air can heal and carry away anything your animal might be holding onto, but ready to release.

Feel the wind blowing through your leaves. Feel your branches swaying to and fro. While staying stable in the earth, you can feel yourself becoming one with the wind. Feel its power to move and expand beyond the past and into a future of healing. See your animal as easily releasing any fears or worries from the past into the wind. See the wind picking up all those things needing to be healed in a swirling and powerful gust, blowing them away, where they dissipate in the healing energy of the universe. Hold this visualization for 20–30 minutes, revisiting the in and out breaths when needed for focus.

Rainbow Heart Connection

Sit quietly for several minutes and connect to the energy of your heart. Breathe in air from the earth into your heart. Visualize your heart as a beautiful center of white light within your being. Imagine this light is filled with all the love and compassion you have experienced in your lifetime. On your out breath, see this light, with all the colors of a rainbow, expanding from your heart, beyond your physical body, into your aura, into the room, and out into the universe.

Next, bring to mind an animal in your life that you would like to connect with for healing in love and compassion. See the energy of the animal's

heart as a beautiful center of white light within his or her being. Expand the rainbow of your heart in love, compassion, serenity, and peace to include the heart of your animal. Remembering that this light is merely an "offering" on your part, and that if the animal is willing your hearts can unify in a beautiful space of healing through this rainbow.

Spiritually, rainbows symbolize hope, harmony, and connection beyond the physical. Visualize your hearts unified in rainbow light and perfectly in balance, at peace, connected, and completely healed. Know that there is no situation that cannot be healed, that there is always hope, and that you will always be connected to each other, no matter what.

CHAPTER SIXTEEN

AFFIRMATIONS

The Power of Affirmations and Staying Positive

> *Your mind is like a piece of land planted with many different kinds of seeds: seeds of joy, peace, mindfulness, understanding, and love; seeds of craving, anger, fear, hate, and forgetfulness. These wholesome and unwholesome seeds are always there, sleeping in the soil of your mind. The quality of your life depends on the seeds you water. If you plant tomato seeds in your gardens, tomatoes will grow. Just so, if you water a seed of peace in your mind, peace will grow. When the seeds of happiness in you are watered, you will become happy. When the seed of anger in you is watered, you will become angry. The seeds that are watered frequently are those that will grow strong. -Thich Nhat Hanh*

It's important to remember, no matter what struggles our animals have, always try to see them as perfect; to do this we need to look not with our eyes but with our hearts.

This isn't about visualizing a physical perfection; it's more about letting go of our eyes, and looking deeper. It's about seeing the animals with our hearts; we need to see the animals as the beautiful bright lights they really are. This light is the inner essence, not the mortal shell, not their physical, emotional struggles. It's so easy to forget this, to instead begin to identify them as their problems on the surface. Remember that underneath the surface, their bright inner light, that is the essence of their being, is already perfect and balanced. If we can see this in them, they will sense it and this will help them remember their inner strength for healing. This is the seed of healing. Remember, our animals are always perfect and bright on the inside, no matter what difficulties they are facing.

Think of affirmations as pure, clean water for these seeds of positivity in the garden of your mind and heart. These affirmations, if you use them frequently, will nurture your consciousness and your ability to stay grounded and balanced. Even when there is chaos around you, affirmations can help you to stay positive. Affirmations and positive thoughts will help you to grow a garden of pure, positive flowers in your mind and heart. Just as a real garden does, this affirmation garden will support the whole community around you!

I will always remember a particular shelter dog that benefitted from affirmations. As I sat with him, I could see he had clearly been neglected in his past. His coat was dull, and his eyes stared blankly into space as he barked continuously. The staff asked me to please try to help calm him, since he had been hysterically barking since he had arrived. I sat quietly outside his kennel, put in my earplugs and took a deep breath. I imagined the energy of the earth flowing up through my body, grounding and centering me. I closed my eyes and inside my mind imagined myself in a quiet, beautiful place.

I added affirmative words: Peace, safety and harmony: I held these three words in my heart. I imagined how the dog would look if he was calm and perfectly relaxed. I imagined I could embrace him with love from my heart. Sure enough, as I've seen in so many Reiki treatments, after a few moments the dog stopped barking and stared intently at me. A few more moments passed and he lay down in the kennel, took a deep breath and rested his head on his front paws. Silence had never felt so golden.

Another great response we can see with affirmations is when working with fearful animals. In these cases it's important to focus on the opposite qualities we are seeing with our eyes and work on holding the positive within us. Rather than fighting against the fear, which actually brings more energy toward the fear itself, we must work to create a strong and clear mental/energetic attitude that is the exact opposite of it. In other words, we must create and hold a foundation of calm, courage and trust within ourselves. We must be a spiritual "rock" of solidity and dependability for our animal.

When we learn to not only visualize, but also *embody* the positive, we can see these kinds of changes in the animals we work with. Dedicated, whole-hearted practice will help us to truly embody this positivity, and the animals will show us when we get there!

Affirmations are very powerful tools for healing. They work best when they are repeated regularly and used often. It is also always best to visualize your affirmation as already having been achieved. In other words, "I am courageous," rather than, "I will be brave soon."

CHAPTER SEVENTEEN

AFFIRMATION MEDITATIONS

Gratitude Affirmation

Sit with the words, "I feel gratitude; each day is a precious gift," inside your heart and body for several minutes. Allow your mind to think about all the people, animals, places and situations in your life for which you are grateful. Alternately, you can focus on the experiences you've had with your animal for which you are grateful, all the parts of his or her unique being for which you are thankful. Feel the meaning and truth of gratitude permeate your whole being—body, mind, emotions and spirit. When you feel encompassed in gratitude within yourself, allow your mind and heart to invite your animal into the space to share this with you.

Clarity and Wisdom Affirmation

Sit with the words, "Clarity in all things. Wisdom in action," inside your heart and body for several minutes. Remember times in your life where you felt clarity and acted wisely based on this clarity. Feel the energy of it permeating your whole being. When you are ready, with your mind and heart, invite your animal to share this beautiful space with you.

Courage Affirmation

Close your eyes and sit comfortably, with the word "courage" inside your heart and body for several minutes. Feel the meaning and truth of that word/emotion permeate your whole being. Imagine what it would look like if your animal were perfectly courageous. See it and then let it go like clouds floating by. When you are ready, open your heart and invite the animal to share that beautiful possibility with you.

Trust Affirmation

Sit with the word trust inside your heart and mind. Feel the meaning and truth of that word/emotion permeate your whole being. Imagine how it would look if your animal felt pure trust at this moment. See it and then let it go like clouds floating by. When you are ready, open your heart and invite your animal to share the space with you.

Peace Affirmation

Close your eyes and sit comfortably with the word peace inside your heart and mind. Feel the meaning and truth of that word/emotion permeate your whole being. Imagine what it would look like if your animal were perfectly peaceful and calm. See it and then let it go like clouds floating by. When you are ready, open your heart and invite your animal to share the peaceful space with you.

CHAPTER EIGHTEEN

SYMPTOMS OF COMPASSION FATIGUE (AND HOW TO COPE)

Did you know that those who work with shelter and sanctuary animals are highly vulnerable to compassion fatigue? Not surprisingly, helping (and opening your heart to) abused, unloved and neglected animals on a regular basis is extremely stressful and traumatic. Those involved in euthanasia of such animals also experience grief. Compassion fatigue, therefore, is unfortunately an occupational hazard for those working with traumatized animals.

According to the Compassion Fatigue Awareness Project (CFAP) and the American Institute of Stress, the symptoms of compassion fatigue vary but can include any of the following:

- Excessive sadness or bottling up of emotions
- Isolating oneself
- Losing your sense of humor
- Neglecting your appearance
- Abusing substances to cope
- Feeling mentally and physically tired
- Having difficulty concentrating
- Reduced sense of meaning or purpose in one's work

If you think you may be suffering from compassion fatigue (but aren't sure), you can start by taking a test found on CFAP's website: http://www.compassionfatigue.org/pages/cfassessment.html.

Healing from compassion fatigue doesn't happen overnight, but there are pro-active steps you can take. CFAP stresses the importance of Self Care during this difficult time and offers the following tips: being kind to yourself, clarifying your personal boundaries, vocalizing your needs and more. The entire list can be found on CFAP's site at http://www.compassionfatigue.org/pages/pathtowellness.html.

Another option is meditation. In my work with animals, I've found that meditating and practicing Reiki can help us to stay centered, strong and balanced amidst all the chaos we observe, sense and feel. If you lack the energy to sustain a long, drawn-out meditation, these mini meditations are a good starting point:

1. **Awaken.** Share this moment with your animal. Check in with your five senses and also your heart (emotion) to help you appreciate all details that exist right now. Tell your animal three things you are grateful for about them.

2. **Ground**. Sit or stand near your animal. Breathe in through your nose filling your entire body with beautiful healing light, all the way to your lower belly. Breathe out and expand this light out of your body and into the universe. Repeat 10 times. Invite your animal into this peaceful space.

3. **Connect**. See your heart as a beautiful light. See your animal's heart as a beautiful light. Imagine your heart can expand out like a rainbow to your animal's heart. Invite them to connect with you in that heart space for healing.

Connecting with the following two Reiki precepts in particular is another way to help guide you down the path to wellness:

1. **Be grateful.** This precept is really about remembering the positive. Sometimes in difficult situations, we forget that every cloud has a silver lining. Figure out what your silver linings are for the animals that you work with. Perhaps a fearful animal you have worked with is showing progress. Maybe an animal who was abandoned finally found a forever family. Even in the case of an animal who died: Were they given kindness in the last moments of their life? Or perhaps their life has illuminated cruelty in a way that will teach and inspire people to help? If we take some time and look deeper

into situations, we can always find things to be grateful for. In fact, some of life's most difficult teachers are also the most profound.

2. **Be honest.** Reach out to fellow rescuers who know what you are going through or to your Reiki friends who share an empathic view of the world. My nonprofit, the Shelter Animal Reiki Association, is a group of more than 400 people around the world who spend time with rescued animals and use the practices of Reiki for support. If you can find people who not only understand, but also offer you a positive and encouraging word, all the better!

   The Reiki precept "be honest" also means understanding your boundaries. What part of your rescue work is the most gratifying? Which parts are the most overwhelming? Spending time becoming more aware of how your time with rescued animals affects your inner state will help you to move toward balance.

CFAP offers a host of resources to help animal caregivers suffering from compassion fatigue. The Wrong Side of the Rainbow (http://shylto4.wix.com/wrongsideofrainbow) also offers information on Self Care as well as links to pet loss forums and a counseling service in Canada. Talking to a therapist can help, too; a simple Google search will lead you to a variety of animal care compassion fatigue specialists, such as Anne Lindsay of TACTdogs.com.

Remember, there is always hope. You are not alone. You are as strong as the earth and as expansive as the sky. All will be well. Take some time to meditate and practice Reiki, and watch both you and the animals you care for shift back into wellness.

CHAPTER NINETEEN

15 REASONS YOU MIGHT BE AN ANIMAL REIKI PRACTITIONER

*Inspired by Jeff Foxworthy's "Reasons You Might Be A Redneck."

1. You love offering Reiki treatments, but the sight of a massage table makes you nervous.

2. After a Reiki treatment, your clothes are often covered in hair and/or drool.

3. Your favorite way to meditate is walking in nature with your dog.

4. Feral animals seem to follow you wherever you go.

5. Your "go to" solution for ant, flea or mouse problems is Reiki.

6. Your cat gets moody if you miss your daily meditation.

7. Your dog lies down at your feet immediately upon hearing Japanese flute music.

8. Your rabbit chooses Reiki over carrots.

9. Your parrot has memorized all of the Reiki chants.

10. You call your pet snake Ssssensei.

11. Alligators aren't scary to you; in fact, they are terrific meditation partners.

12. You missed the fireworks this year because you were meditating with your animals.

13. Your dog doesn't fetch the newspaper; he fetches a paper listing the 5 Precepts whenever you seem stressed.

14. You learned the meaning of the Buddhist term "monkey mind" from a real monkey.

15. Your horse handed you a blue ribbon when you finally learned to just "let go and let Reiki."

CHAPTER TWENTY

THREE REASONS ANIMAL REIKI ROCKS!

There are so many reasons to love Reiki for animals! Those of us who have been practicing for a long time (or even a short time) know this well. But next time you find yourself talking to someone about why you love it, keep in mind some of these mainstream reasons why it's the GO TO method for supporting yourself, animals, people and the planet!

In a nutshell, Animal Reiki Rocks because...

1. It's About Healing Touch

According to the University of Minnesota, research indicates that touch has the power to relieve pain, reduce stress, fatigue, depression, and anxiety as well as manage the symptoms of cancer treatments and post-operative pain and recovery.

2. It's About Animal Connections

According to Duke Cancer Institute, animal assisted therapy is a highly effective form of intervention which improves moods and energy, decreases pain and anxiety and "has not only been shown to aid stress and depression, but provides a sense of companionship that can combat feelings of isolation. It is a cheap yet effective way to maximize health outcomes for hospital patients."

3. It's About Meditation—and Meditation Works, even Science agrees!

According to the Mayo Clinic, meditation is a "simple, fast way to reduce stress." Research suggests that meditation helps people to manage health conditions such as anxiety, cancer, depression, heart disease, pain and more.

Reiki as a healing touch practice.

Two parts of the system of Reiki incorporate touch: self-treatment and treatment of others. Reiki practitioners are taught formal hand positions to use when doing Reiki on themselves, as well as hand positions for offering Reiki to humans. When offering to animals, touch is optional and animal-initiated. Because we are very tactile creatures, we humans feel support and compassion in a very direct way through touch. Clients often describe feelings of relaxation, harmony and well-being after a Reiki treatment. Sometimes this is also the case for animals, although some animals may be too sensitive for touch therapy in Reiki. Thus touch is an important part of the system of Reiki, however as Reiki is also effective off the body, this can be adapted to the comfort level of each individual.

Reiki as an animal therapy practice.

When offering Reiki to animals, practitioners find an amazing result— often they see that animals are healing us even though we may initially think we are there to help them heal. This is a result of the beautiful gift of animal presence. Just being in the presence of animals is healing— connecting with them through petting, speaking or even just gentle presence has an immediate healing effect on us. This is because animals are fully present, without expectation, judgment and agenda. They accept us unconditionally as we are and this causes our hearts to open without us even trying (and sometimes without us even being aware of it). It is when our hearts are open that healing can truly begin.

Reiki as a meditative practice.

Reiki is a system of spiritual practice that utilizes five elements (according to the International House of Reiki):

    The Reiki Precepts
    Traditional Breathing Practices
    Healing Treatments
    Symbols and Mantras
    Initiations

If we take a deeper look at each of these five elements, we can see the heart is to create a meditative state of mind. When working with the precepts, the key is to contemplate them in a meditative way so that we can go deeper into their meaning and purpose in our everyday lives, bringing change and healing to all that we do. When working with the breathing practices, the key is to follow the breath into a meditative space where healing can happen. As a practitioner, when we offer a healing treatment to a person or animal, the key is that we go deeper into a meditative state of mind so that we can support the healing process. When practicing the symbols and mantras, either through contemplation or chanting, we learn that they are tools to help us to release our busy mind and find our inner "still point"–or inner meditative space to facilitate healing. And finally, as a teacher, when offering initiations to our students, the key is to create a meditative space within ourselves and within the ritual to support the student's healing process. Both teachers and practitioners of the system of Reiki often describe how their meditation practice has changed their lives— from the inside out—and made their world a better and more peaceful place.

Thus we can see that every part of the system of Reiki is ultimately about meditation as a doorway to healing. While some people may not have heard of Reiki, everyone longs for a peaceful, harmonious and stress-free life. So why not ROCK your world—and the world of those around you—by sharing with others how animal Reiki practice helps YOU!

CHAPTER TWENTY-ONE

REIKI IS WISDOM AND COMPASSION

For we did not weave the web of life. We are merely a strand in it. Whatever we do to the web, we do to ourselves. Let us give thanks for the web and the circle that connects us. -Chief Seattle

Sometimes when I fly, I get very philosophical. Just the other day, I was sitting in a plane, and suddenly became aware of how much of my life depends on others. I was thinking about the pilot flying the plane, the flight attendants looking after all of us passengers, the cooperation of all of the passengers to make it a safe and pleasant experience. I looked at my seatbelt, the chair in front of me, my cup of water, and all the other parts of the plane around me and reflected on the many, many people it took to make this plane trip happen. For me to be sitting there at that moment, it took the attention and care of engineers, artists, designers, mechanics, safety experts and more... People who had probably spent years studying their craft, and in turn, who owed their own learning and expertise to countless other individuals. I felt a surge of gratitude at that moment, and felt myself surrounded by the energy of many caring people who shared their talents with the world so that people could travel through the air. How amazing and generous is that?! It just made me want to smile and help everyone I saw.

I guess Albert Einstein, even though he was a scientist, ruminated on this spiritual truth a lot in his life:

A hundred times a day I remind myself that my inner and outer life depends on the labor of other people, living and dead, and that I must exert myself in order to give in the same measure as I have received and am still receiving. I am strongly drawn to the simple life and am often oppressed by the feeling that I am engrossing an unnecessary amount of labor of my fellow people.

It is this wisdom, the realization of this interdependence of all beings (including animals and mother nature too) that nurtures and deepens compassion in each of us. For me, it is my work with Reiki and animals which brings wisdom of the interconnectedness of all things to the surface of my awareness on a daily basis, and thus reminds me that compassion makes the world go 'round. And more than that: compassion heals. As Lama Zopa Rinpoche says, "A person with loving kindness and compassion heals others simply by existing."

So what exactly is Reiki? In the deepest sense, Reiki, very simply, IS wisdom and compassion. Therefore, Reiki heals. Let's look at the elements of the system of Reiki and see how wisdom and compassion fit in...

We can see from the Precepts—For today only: Do not anger, do not worry, be humble, be honest, be compassionate—that compassion is directly stated as a precept for living a balanced life. The other precepts are steps to help us access our compassion; the more that we let go of anger, worry and ego, and the more we can uncover our true inner wisdom—the realization that we are all interconnected—and thus naturally arises compassion! Practicing the precepts with the animals also helps us remember our wisdom by dissolving species differences and revealing spiritual oneness. In my experience, animals help teach us the precepts and open the door to our inner compassion.

We can also see wisdom and compassion in the traditional practices and meditations taught in the system of Reiki, for example the Joshin Kokyu Ho. In this breathing meditative practice, the person sits quietly and brings their energy in through their nose, filling their body with healing light, all the way to the Hara (the energy center below the navel). On the exhale, the person expands this light out in all directions, infinitely in the universe. By connecting with the Hara, our energy becomes more centered, more grounded, yet at the same time more connected to the entire universe. In essence, with each breath, we are gathering our energy and stabilizing ourselves energetically, while sharing ourselves with all. This is not something we can do with our intellectual mind, rather it is a practice for the body and spirit, and our mind can just relax. By letting go of the mind, and focusing on the breath (which bridges body and spirit), we can slowly let go of anger, worry, and ego; thus again we are remembering our inner wisdom, our connection to all things—and in this space compassion naturally arises. I find that this practice of Joshin Kokyu Ho is best practiced with our animals, as they are great meditation partners! Because they connect with the world and spirit beyond the intellectual mind, they help us too, to go deeper.

We can also see wisdom and compassion in the symbols and the mantras. Practicing with the visual aid of the symbols, or the verbal/sound practice of the mantras engages our sight, our speech and our breath. Just as with the breathing practices, the symbols and mantras help us to let go of mind chatter and sit in a more quiet mental place, while supporting an inner energetic focus on the path towards wisdom: grounding, a nurturing of mental harmony and a state of mind of oneness. An inner drive to compassionate action is a natural by-product of our work with the symbols and mantras. Again, invite your animals to sit with you as you work with the symbols and mantras, they will support you to go deeper!

We can also see wisdom and compassion in our Reiki treatments with others. When we sit and share a Reiki space with a person or an animal, we must be truly present. Hopefully we have a daily meditation practice to help us to heal our own issues—it's important to work with our own anger, worry and ego—in order to be able to hold a space of compassion. To be with another being, with an open heart, with a listening spirit, with a humble eye, to truly become "*one*," this is our expression of wisdom and compassion as Reiki practitioners. It is not that we are doing something "*to*" them, rather that we are sharing and "*being*." This is how we can really help and support others in their healing journeys. In essence, a Reiki practitioner strives to be a bodhisattva, and this is something anyone can do. For me, animals are the greatest bodhisattvas!

> *A bodhisattva is someone who has compassion within himself or herself and who is able to make another person smile or help someone suffer less. Every one of us is capable of this.* -Thich Nhat Hanh

We can also see wisdom and compassion in our energetic connection with our Reiki teachers—symbolized by the ritual of Reiju (initiations or attunements) they share with us. In creating a compassionate space and connection with their students through Reiju, Reiki teachers can help their students rediscover their inner wisdom—knowledge of the oneness with all things—and secondly, help their students to open more deeply to manifesting this through compassionate actions in everyday life. In essence, Reiju is simply a ritual to nurture and grow wisdom and compassion! As Buddhist teacher John Daido Loori said:

> *Know that deep within each and every one of us, under layers of conditioning, there is an enlightened being, alive and well. In order to function, it needs to be discovered. To discover this Buddha is wisdom. To make it function in the world is compassion. That wisdom and compassion is the life of each one of us. It is up to you what you do with it.*

Our highest goal in practicing Reiki is realizing we are all one (wisdom) and acting upon this in service to others (compassion). Reiki is Japanese in origin and we can see this reflected in the individual teachings and practices, however, this wisdom and compassion is a universal truth that we can see in all main spiritual practices around the globe. It transcends culture, politics, religion, society, species and even time. The ancient text of the Bhagavad-Gita says, "*When a person responds to the joys and sorrows of others as if they were his own, he has attained the highest state of spiritual union.*" And although some may say, "*Wisdom and compassion, is that all that Reiki is? Isn't it something more?*" To that I say, truly, what more is there?

CHAPTER TWENTY-TWO

THE REIKI GIFTS OF HEALING: EARTH AND SKY

People usually consider walking on water or in thin air a miracle. But I think the real miracle is not to walk either on water or in thin air, but to walk on earth. Every day we are engaged in a miracle which we don't even recognize: a blue sky, white clouds, green leaves, the black, curious eyes of a child—our own two eyes. All is a miracle. -Thich Nhat Hanh

I love this quote because it helps us to remember what a miracle life is! For me, my animal Reiki practice is something that brings magic and miracles to my life every single day.

The meditative gifts of animal Reiki practice are many, however I'd like to focus on the gifts of healing brought by connecting to the earth and sky. For me, the earth and sky are at the core of many Reiki practices because they are two of the purest qualities of our spiritual essence, and as such are keys to our wellness. To touch earth and sky energy within one's own nature is to access the ability to relieve suffering and find healing in the deepest layers of being. Earth and sky practice brings balance, peace and harmony. Our animals can also benefit from our self-practice; when we invite them into this space of wellbeing and harmony, we can support their self-healing too.

The Stable Healing of Earth: Remembering Where We Come From

The clearest way into the Universe is through a forest wilderness. – John Muir

It's true; a forest is a wonderful place to rediscover the universe inside us. Connecting with forests or other natural places on earth brings the gifts of grounding and stability. This happens more easily when we develop our connection to our Hara with regular Reiki practice. In reality, since we are physical beings, we come from the earth and we will also return to it once we die. Everything we have in this life—our breath, our health, our food, our water and more—we owe in one way or another to her generosity and wisdom.

Even so, perhaps it is human nature to take life for granted. We imagine that we will always have the gifts that earth provides. And then one day, when we come face to face with our mortality—when we realize that in truth, at any moment it all could end—then suddenly the most mundane earthly things become the most miraculous and beautiful—the laugh of our child, the click of our dog's toenails on the floor, a flower or sunset.

Out the windows of my home I can see a natural temple made of earth— Mount Tamalpais, a beautiful mountain here in Marin County where I live. For many ages she has been here, standing so proud and tall. I love that I get to see this mountain at all times of the day, for she looks different at sunrise than she does in midday or at sunset. I love that I get to see her in all kinds of weather—shining in the sun or obscured by clouds. Through the wind and rain, sometimes I can catch a glimpse of her. And even in the darkest night, although I can't see her, I know my mountain is always there.

One day my world changed as I knew it—I was diagnosed with breast cancer and I knew it would take everything I had inside of me, including the grace of the universe, to survive. Suddenly I realized, on a deep visceral level, that life had absolutely no guarantees—not even tomorrow—and all I had was this very moment in time. As soon as I got home from the hospital after my diagnosis, my whole being was drawn to look out the window, and I remember standing there silently, gazing at her tall, dark form, as everything inside of me felt as if it were crumbling.

As I looked out my window it was as if I had new and different eyes, and I suddenly saw something in this mountain that gave me resolve: the strength and stability of earth—dependable, immoveable, unemotional. As I moved through my surgery, treatments and recovery, she watched, silent and strong. Some days I would feel so weak and mortal, as if the slightest breeze could dissipate my energy and I simply would cease to exist. On these hardest, most painful or scary days, I would lie in the guest bedroom where I could see the mountain from my pillow and ask her for healing. I would imagine that all of her strength and fortitude was also inside of me. We are not so different, I would say to her; you and I, we are both made of earth. Her unchanging presence—a powerful symbol of earth's power—was an incredible comfort to me, and helped me to weather the storming emotions that the coming months would bring.

Experiencing this stability in myself was such a gift from the earth, and it gave me insight into many animal experiences I had had over the years. For example, when working with traumatized horses, often I would feel their energy as very flighty, unstable and chaotic. To place my own energy in their space, it would take lots of focus on grounding, so that I wasn't also swept away into their chaos and fear. The horses had shown me over the years that by turning inward, focusing on my Hara, feeling the earth beneath my feet and its stability inside of me, I would experience an interesting change. Even the most unstable of horses would eventually stop his fretting, take notice of me, sometimes even coming over to investigate and connect. Over and over I would see that as soon as I got my own grounding, the horse would also slow down, relax, and maybe even sleep. And even when they chose to continue to move around and graze during treatment, there would be such a big shift into calmness that I could sense in their energy. It was as if they had felt the earth inside of me, and then remembered it inside of themselves. Although I had experienced this with many horses over the years, the fact that these were gifts from the earth eluded me until I had experienced this grounding and strength in my own healing journey.

The Spacious Healing of Sky: Remembering Our Expansive Spirit

The gift of the sky represents the spacious nature of our relaxed consciousness. This happens when we let go of our thoughts and intellectual mind and just sit in the perfect stillness of the Reiki space. So many times in our lives we are focusing on regrets in the past, worries about the future, or trying to control the present moment—our minds are so busy "doing" that we forget about "being!" Buddhism teaches that happiness is when we learn to let go without judgment into the spaciousness of our mind:

Vast and spacious as the sky, this is our mind without the dualistic labeling. When we label and get attached to dualistic thoughts our mind becomes cluttered, boxed in, and narrow. When we can naturally experience this openness of mind without effort this is the process. Having the ability to sustain and maintain this vastness of mind, this spaciousness mind and clarity of mind in all situations in life is called Perfect Happiness. -Chukdong

But what if this present moment is difficult? When going through a challenge such as a life-threatening illness, we might find our thoughts slowly getting more and more focused on our problems. Dwelling on our physical suffering, worrying about the pain and side-effects of treatments and surgeries, fears about if/when we will recover—these kinds of thoughts become like thick clouds covering the vast nature of our mind. Sometimes it might feel like we ARE the disease, and that there is nothing but pain, fear or a bad ending—our minds become smaller and more boxed in, darker and more depressed.

For me, Reiki chanting was the practice that helped my mind to let go of all the clouds of fear and suffering, that helped me to remember who I really am. In reality, my inner essence is eternal, is bright, is beautiful, is perfect, is connected to all things and is as wide as the universe. My true essence is always free and always well. After a chanting session, I could always feel this spiritual shift inside of me, no matter what I was going through physically. Maybe the pain was still there, maybe I still had some fear, but it no longer felt overwhelming, or as if that was ALL there was. I could sense and feel so much more possibility within myself—compassion as wide as the universe, healing potential as deep as forever. This recognition of my larger spiritual self gave me so much relief and comfort from my suffering...

It also made me suddenly mindful of the experiences of shelter animals I had offered Reiki to over the years. These were animals who were frightened, abused or traumatized. Some of them were suffering terrible injuries or illnesses, even dying, yet when I would sit with them in the Reiki space, and allow my mind to let go—completely let go of worries, fears, judgments, expectations, all of it—then, as I felt my mind relax, I would see that even the animals with the most suffering would be able to lie down peacefully, take a deep sigh, and truly relax. The reality of being in a shelter hadn't changed, their health hadn't changed (yet—but often healing or adoption miracles do shortly follow treatments!) and yet they were able to find peace and wellbeing even in the midst of that difficult

situation. What a miracle! I had witnessed this so many times over the years, but it was only after I had experienced the expansion and letting go in my consciousness during my own deep suffering that I recognized these were the gifts of the sky.

Pondering all of these experiences, I've come to realize that although Reiki often lessens pain and improves physical or mental issues, it's not always that Reiki necessarily removes the suffering, but it just puts it in perspective. Suffering might be there, yes, but it's not the only thing that is there; it's not the only thing that we are. I suppose we could say that suffering is part of life, but the question is, do we let ourselves be overwhelmed by it? If we can stay grounded and stable, while also finding a way to touch our expansive consciousness, suffering loses its strong grip and we can find our way back to balance.

For me that's the real gift of Reiki—not that it will prevent anything bad from ever happening to us—there are always bumps in the road of life— however Reiki can help us to stay in touch with our true natures, which always and at every moment, no matter what we are facing, have the capacity to experience peace, harmony and relief from suffering.

Developing the earth and sky together within our bodies through the practices of Reiki brings peace, equanimity, balance and perfect, lasting healing—beyond the physical body; it is the healing of our eternal spirit. This peacefulness is always there, no matter what struggles we or our animals will face. Grounding in the earth and letting ourselves expand into the sky allows us to remember our true natures. Our Reiki practice gives us the tools to uncover our inner bright light that is always perfect and beautiful, no matter what struggles we, or our animals, may face on the surface.

CHAPTER TWENTY-THREE

EXPLORING REIKI AND COMPASSION WITH THE EXOTIC ANIMALS OF CARE

Compassion is a beautiful light that comes from your personal practice. Just sit back, relax and open yourself up. Be that sun that shines. The sun does not make any judgment; it's just shining away. Pure compassion. And from this the animal takes whatever it needs. -Frans Stiene, The International House of Reiki

Compassion and Reiki: Where does one end and the other begin? A recent trip to Apopka, Florida, to teach Reiki at the CARE Foundation, a sanctuary for exotic wildlife such as alligators, bears, tigers and panthers, helped me to understand more fully compassion as a concept within the system of Reiki.

My visit to CARE made for an awe-inspiring animal Reiki adventure, thanks to the wisdom of the animal teachers, the receptivity of the people to what the animals had to teach, the amazing responses of the animals to the energy—not to mention the beauty of the surroundings. Upon my return, I realized that what I have taken most from the animals there is a deeper lesson in what it is to practice compassion, and to be Reiki with an animal, rather than do Reiki to an animal. It is this openness of approach that helps facilitate interspecies Reiki connections and create a beautiful and deep healing experience. This experience also goes two ways: humans healing animals, and animals healing humans. Following are some of the highlights and profound experiences I encountered while working with the amazing animals living at the CARE Foundation.

Pre-Trip Prep

In the weeks leading up to the class, I knew it would be a beautiful experience to meet with these animals, but also a difficult one. On the one hand, what a privilege to connect with these majestic and powerful creatures, but on the other hand, we would have to confront the dark side of mankind's ignorance and mistakes firsthand. All of these animals are captive, rather than running free in the wild as they should be. All had suffered and perhaps still were suffering in one way or another. I knew also, for this same reason, that it would be a challenge for my students, who were traveling from all over the country to be a part of this class.

I began to meditate for strength to hold a calm, strong space for all of us to be present, humans and animals alike. I asked the universe to support the weekend so that lessons and healing could go both ways for everyone present who was of open heart. As a Reiki teacher, for many weeks leading up to my visit, I felt the great depth of responsibility in holding a space of Reiki healing for everyone as we spent these Reiki days together. I focused on my own personal spiritual practice in daily Reiki as a way to provide an anchor and foundation for me to be able to help facilitate the healing experience.

Déjà Vu ...

Finally, after months of preparation, I was there! Walking through the grounds of the CARE Foundation, just a day before teaching my first class there, felt oddly familiar. As I wound my way through the trees to each of the animal enclosures, visiting the bears, leopards, alligators, tigers, monkeys and many more species of animals, I suddenly remembered—I had been dreaming of walking through these woods for several weeks. These very woods with these very animals! A wave of déjà vu swept over me.

As I stepped up to the cage that housed Mokoto, a beautiful and intense black leopard, I locked eyes with him and saw a familiar face: I was sure I had dreamed of him in particular. He was so familiar that it felt a bit eerie. "I remember you," I said to him. In response, Mokoto turned his back to me and rubbed his head against the fence, making small meowing and purring sounds. Just like the tamest, most loving little kitty-cat. This was a "man eater" who was so very dangerous? I thought of the Reiki precept, *For today only, do not anger.* With Mokoto's invitation, I sat down and began to connect with him through Reiki, and within a few minutes he had turned upside-down, pushing his hind feet against the fence and hanging his head off the edge of the ledge, eyes shut and breathing deeply. For my own part, the energetic connection felt trance-like. Deep darkness, intense light, full of peace and yet empty of everything. I forgot where I was for several minutes and allowed myself to be carried away with Mokoto into the Reiki space.

After meeting with Christin Burford and Travis DeVita, director and co-director, respectively, of CARE, and taking a tour of their incredible facility, I was surprised at the energy that I kept feeling—gratitude. I had expected to experience sadness or frustration from the animals, as I often do when visiting shelters and sanctuaries around the country, but here was simply the strong feeling of thanks, as if the animals knew, due to their prior experiences, that only "through grace have we arrived here at this safe haven. We are the lucky ones."

The CARE Foundation

The CARE Foundation is a nonprofit organization that provides permanent sanctuary for non-releasable wildlife and other animals. The animals at CARE have come from a variety of backgrounds, but most of them share a past wrought with difficulties due to human ignorance, neglect and/or abuse. CARE also provides a variety of educational programs and public appearances throughout the community. The primary goals of these programs are conservation and animal safety. Christin and Travis, who also live on the property, dedicate their lives completely to the animals in their care. They are truly an inspiration!

Although they had little knowledge of Reiki, Christin and Travis welcomed my Reiki students, Leah (my partner and co-founder of the Shelter Animal Reiki Association) and me with open arms into their facility. "We're open to anything that can help our animals," Christin shared with me. Both Christin and Travis also decided to get trained in Reiki to help their animals!

The Alligators and Crocodile Tears

On the afternoon of the second day of class, as students scattered to do treatments with various snakes, birds, monkeys and other wild creatures, I decided to sit with the alligators. No one had done Reiki with the four gators—Bubba, Boris, Brutus and Tiny—yet. They sat like stones in their enclosures as I sat nearby, facing slightly away from them so as not to bother their rest. Although they didn't move, I knew they were very aware of my presence and also very intent upon discovering my reason for sitting with them.

After a few minutes of offering Reiki to them, I began to feel a heaviness in my legs and arms. The energy began to flow very strongly, and I realized the alligators were very open to connecting with Reiki. My body began to feel like lead, as if I was magnetized to the earth. It felt as if I wasn't just "connecting" with earth energy, but rather experiencing what it felt to "be" earth energy. Ancient and wise, these alligators were teaching me how to create a solid foundation. The Reiki precept, *For today only, do not worry,* came to my mind. There was such a calm strength in their energy. Such confidence. At the same time, I began to realize that my awareness of my surroundings was becoming much more acute. I sensed a person walking silently behind me. By my sensing of their energy, it was if they were right behind me, but when I turned my head to look, they were more than 100 feet away. Alligators are, I realized at that moment, the perfect meditators. Still as stones, but completely and totally present in the moment—aware of all that is going on around them. Again I wondered, who is giving whom Reiki?

Later that day, one of the students in the class, Sue, shared her own reptile Reiki experience with me:

> I decided to go see Ingozi the crocodile again, since we seemed to connect when he came over to me during our Reiki session earlier in the day. It was so weird. I was walking up to his pen, feeling completely normal, and all of the sudden tears just started flowing out of me really hard. I wasn't feeling sad, it just happened. I still don't know why it happened. I told him goodbye and that I'd connect to him through distance Reiki. He bounced his head up and down on his platform. I thought that was so cool.

Who would have imagined a crocodile to be so open to Reiki and even to be a healer? It was truly humbling to realize that the animals here were helping all of us perhaps even more than we were helping them. Imagine that!

The Heart of the Bear

As I walked up to the black bear named Quinn, I noticed he looked quite hot and uncomfortable. His back was to me, and he lay sprawled over the huge rubber tire in his enclosure. Well, yes, it was a sticky day, but here it was only February, and I couldn't imagine how hot he must be in the summer! Well, luckily he had a nice swimming pool in there to help him keep cool. Clearly, he was quite bored by my arrival, choosing to totally ignore me.

As I began to offer him Reiki, I held an open mind about whether or not he would choose to connect with me—either way was fine by me. As the energy began to flow, almost immediately I felt a strong heat around my heart. Love. Just like the heart of a big teddy bear that you spent your childhood hugging, that is what it felt like. Simple and honest, yet also old, solid and grounded. Suddenly I had the image of his favorite person, Travis, who helps Christin run the sanctuary. Love. Travis. Love. Travis. The feeling of gratitude washed over me, yet again. Yes, Quinn, I hear you. I visualized my meeting with Travis the day before, our wonderful conversation, our hug as we parted ways. Immediately Quinn lifted his head and stared at me. He then got up and came right over to the fence, eyeing me from the side. As if to say, "Yes, that's him, yep, Travis, isn't he wonderful? Where is he? Can you get him? I miss him so. Can he come visit me?" I promised him I would give Travis the message and sat a few more minutes in the beautiful heart energy that just is Quinn. If he was a little bear, I would have been tempted to hold him in my lap like a baby. So strong yet what a squishy heart that big guy has! The Reiki precept, "Be honest in your work", came to my mind. How beautiful is the work of Christin and Travis, as they devote all day every day in caring for these animals. How beautiful, too, the honesty of emotion and connection that Quinn was willing to share with me, and that he shares with his special person.

The Spirit of the Tiger

Sitting in front of Bahl-shoy, a beautiful, orange Siberian tiger, was, I admit, a bit intimidating. Even with the double chain-link fence. Just the sheer diameter of his front legs was a marvel. I suddenly became acutely aware of my waifish human appearance and delicate physical nature. What must it be like to be housed in such armor as this?

As I closed my eyes and asked him to connect with me, I found myself going very deep. The pull of the energy was so strong it was nothing like I have ever felt before. Like a magnet, pulling me out of my body, taking me so deeply away and yet at the same time so deeply into the core of myself that I lost all time and space for several moments. When I opened my eyes, he was lying peacefully on a ledge, breathing deeply and gazing lazily at me. As we met eyes, he roused himself and walked down off his platform and over to the fence to me, chuffing a greeting, "Prrr.... Prrr." As if to say, "Yes, you got it, that's what it's like to have a tiger's spirit. And I feel what it is to be you, too, and I thank you for sharing that with me." The Reiki precept came to me, Be humble. Bahl-shoy manifested this precept perfectly. He was just true to himself, without regret, without apology. He was present in the moment and open to connecting with me, even though I was just a stranger asking to share a deeper space. How humbling it was to be able to be in the presence of, and connect energetically to, such a majestic creature. As I thanked him and walked away, I was overcome again with the emotion of gratitude that seemed to encompass all the animals I was connecting with. I wondered again to myself, after all, who is giving whom Reiki here?

Gratitude was again the theme when one of the students from the class, Kim, shared her own Reiki experience with another tiger named Tigger:

> *I didn't realize it until I went to sit down that Tigger was lying less than five feet from me under a platform in the shade. I didn't show it, but I was a little startled to see him right in front of me. I didn't know until later that he was nearly starved to death before coming to CARE and there was doubt as to whether he would survive. Well, thank goodness he did; he is beautiful.*
>
> *I said hello to them and got settled in my chair. Tigger became so relaxed that I had no fear with him so close. I actually told him that I wished I could crawl in there with him. I told him how grateful I was that he had survived his life to make it to CARE because if he wasn't there, I wouldn't be seeing him, and I was grateful for that. Suddenly there was an explosion of green light as our hearts connected in a green ball. I can't describe it any differently. It was so amazing, and waves of gratitude and love washed over me. I actually teared up. When I opened my eyes and said thank you to him for the incredible experience, I asked if I could take his picture. He looked at me and gave me a big Reiki yawn, which I caught just in time. I couldn't believe it.*

Lessons Beyond the Class

> *Mokoto's eyes burned through me: "Look deeper, I am more than my captivity. Look deeper, I am more than my past. Look deeper, I am more than my present and my future. Look. You will see it." I felt my heart opening, and indeed I could see. Suffering. Gratitude. Strength. Light.*

I awoke with a strong vibration of energy still resounding within my chest. In that moment, with the energy of Mokoto still resonating through me, I could feel what it means to practice compassion. Gratitude was the message the animals were sending over and over to us throughout the weekend. And at that moment, I could see that gratitude is only one side of the coin. Suffering is the other. To have experienced a deep level of suffering, as all of these animals have in one way or another, is to be able to experience even more gratitude in the present moment. When we can be present with the animals in their suffering, and even more deeply in their gratitude, we can experience true compassion. We can experience what Reiki is. In addition, when we can also begin to look at our own suffering while also becoming more mindful of things in our life to be grateful for, then the doors of compassion and healing can truly open to our self-healing. The animals were simply a mirror for our own journey into healing. Perhaps the deepest lesson from the animals at CARE was a deeper understanding of the Reiki precept, Be compassionate to yourself and others. And for me, in many ways, the animals have shown me that yes, indeed, Reiki and compassion are one and the same.

Postscript

We all noticed how relaxed the animals were after the Reiki classes—for example, rolling on their backs with all four feet in the air or just sacked out, sleeping. Soon after the class, Christin gave a tour of the facility for her veterinarian and many of his friends. It was feeding time, and the tigers usually put up quite a show of fierceness and growling in front of all the people. Well, Christin couldn't wait to tell us—she was amazed— the tigers didn't even growl once; they just looked calmly at the large group of visitors and then lay down to eat their dinners peacefully. She said she had never seen anything like it!

CHAPTER TWENTY-FOUR

FIVE REIKI LESSONS FROM MY ANIMAL TEACHERS

Animals. It's always been about the animals for me. As long as I can remember, there has always been an animal in my life, at my side, walking with me through thick and thin. Animals have always been my best friends, and since I was a little girl, I have understood them well—in fact, often better than my fellow humans. When I initially learned Reiki as a tool for self-healing, it was my own dog, Dakota, who first helped me make the connection between Reiki and animals. He would lie awkwardly across my feet whenever I did a Reiki self-practice. One day it dawned on me: He senses Reiki. Which led me to the next conclusion: He knows Reiki can help him. Which led me to the next realization: Of his own choice, he is coming forward and accepting Reiki. I had almost nothing to do with it (other than sitting in a Reiki meditation myself), and yet he seemed to know exactly what was going on—not only was he participating in the energy healing treatment, he had taken it over for his own purposes. This series of "light bulb" moments proved to be the beginning of what would become an eventual career change for me, from middle school teacher to animal Reiki teacher, and the beginning of a life mission to bring Reiki to animals around the world.

It has been my great honor and privilege along the way to call many animals of many different species my Reiki teachers. Of course, I've got my human Reiki teachers, too, and they have been an invaluable part of my journey. However, it has been when sitting with the animals, in that quiet peace that is Reiki, where I have learned my most profound lessons about the nature of this "energy" that is Reiki. In this article, I'd like to share just a few.

One of my clients was a kitty in a multiple cat household with a very caring and concerned human guardian. I was brought in to offer Reiki to this particular kitty, but he wasn't too keen on the treatment at first, so I decided to get creative to see if I could find a way he would accept the energy. First, I decided to include the other kitties as well in the treatment, which the other cats really appreciated, but he still wasn't into it. As he sat staring at me in an annoyed way, I suddenly got the strong impression that he wanted his person to get healing. Although she was a Reiki practitioner herself, she didn't often "do animals" and normally waited in the other room during treatments. I decided to ask her to sit in and meditate with all of us during the treatment. I couldn't believe the difference this made! As soon as he saw his person sit down with us and open to the energy, the cat came right up to me, licked my hands and then settled down with his person for a long Reiki nap. She, too, was astounded by the change in his attitude and delighted by the feeling of being together with her cats in the peaceful Reiki space. She decided that self-practice (with her cats free to join in) should be a regular tradition.

This story illustrates Animal Reiki Lesson 1: Always start by healing yourself. Although many of us find Reiki because of our desire to help someone we love (either human or animal), the key and cornerstone of the system is self-practice. It's easy to forget this and become depleted as caretakers in times of illness, injury or hospice. It's important to remember that our effectiveness and ability to truly offer healing to another being is directly affected by our own connection to the energy. Make friends with Reiki; make it not just a part of your life, but part of everything you do. Become Reiki, and in that space you will find that everywhere you go you will be able to offer a space for others in which to find balance and harmony.

Take the case of a particular cat whose Reiki person sadly lamented to me, "Here I am a full-time Reiki practitioner, and my own cat hates Reiki!" When asking her how she went about the treatment, I discovered she always picked up her cat, placed him on her lap and began the treatment. Within a minute or less, the cat inevitably jumped off her lap and ran quickly from the room. When she would be treating her human clients, however, interestingly, the cat was always in the room, sleeping soundly.

I asked her to try something different: to find a comfortable place in her house to sit in meditation and set her intention to be open to facilitate healing for her cat if he was open for Reiki (otherwise he didn't need to take any Reiki at all). I told her to simply sit in the Reiki energy for 30 minutes, not worrying about what he was doing, where he was, how he was responding, if he was "taking" it and so on. In other words, I asked for her to simply sit in a Reiki meditation in her own space.

Within several minutes of beginning the treatment, she opened her eyes to find her cat sitting at her feet staring intently at her. Instead of reacting, she simply closed her eyes again and continued to offer the energy. Her cat lay quietly at her feet in a "Reiki nap" for several minutes. By the end of the treatment, her cat jumped into her lap and proceeded to rub his head against her hands, turning his body this way and that so as to direct her hands where he preferred them to be for treatment.

This treatment was a turning point for their Reiki relationship. Her cat now comes to her and "demands" his Reiki treatments on a regular basis! Sometimes he sits in her lap, and sometimes he sleeps across the room, absorbing the energy from a distance. But most importantly, it is his decision, not hers.

This story illustrates Animal Reiki Lesson 2: Let animals control the treatment. Trust the energy to go where it needs to go. You don't need to use hands-on contact. Even if this is more comfortable for us, it often is unacceptable for animals. To receive the best possible acceptance and openness from the animals, never initiate a hands-on Reiki treatment; always let the animal be the one to decide to come forward for hands-on Reiki if he or she so chooses. Remember that hands-off treatment is just as effective, and in fact more so, in that you will most of the time receive more openness from the animal without hands-on contact.

One of the guide dogs I worked with had a terrible case of kennel anxiety. He was so unhappy, in fact, that they wondered if he would be able to make it through the training to see graduation day. He had become so worked up in the kennel that he was unable to focus on his training program. When he first entered the treatment room, he was highly keyed up and agitated. Within a few minutes as I offered Reiki, the dog relaxed completely, lying halfway in my lap and going deeply into a "Reiki nap."

I suddenly had a strong sensation of loud barking, and at the same time physical pain in my ears and a feeling of being completely overwhelmed by the noise. It became suddenly clear to me that this was the experience of this highly sensitive dog in the kennel environment. I shared my experiences during the treatment with the dog's caretaker, who in turn worked with the dog's trainers to change his program. Besides taking the dog out of the kennel area during the particularly active and loud times of the day, they began to stuff his ears with cotton during the times where he had to remain in a noisy area. Immediately they began to see a reduction in stress and an improved ability to focus on the training at hand.

This story illustrates Animal Reiki Lesson 3: Listen to your intuition. Sometimes when we are connected to an animal during a Reiki treatment, we may suddenly understand something very important about the animal or his situation. We may be in a unique position to advocate for that animal. Ask yourself if sharing this information will bring healing and help to the animal: If the answer is an unequivocal "yes," then share your intuitive information.

Another of my students was new to Reiki. One day her horse was uncomfortable, but she couldn't isolate the problem area, and, not fully trusting her ability to offer healing to him, felt very helpless. I asked her to offer Reiki to her horse with me. I guided her through setting of intention and asking permission, reminding her simply to connect with the energy and allow her horse to set the tone of the treatment. It was a beautiful thing to watch the connection between this horse and his person within the Reiki space. Within a few minutes, the horse lifted his head and looked at her, clearly asking for her to do some hands-on Reiki. As she placed her hands on his shoulder, the most incredible thing took place: The horse began to shake his skin over and over, literally moving her hands upward and backward across his back toward his hind end. At a certain point he stopped his skin movement, settling into deep relaxation. She felt heat and pain in her hands from this area of his body. She realized he had guided her to his problem spot! The next day she shared with me that not only had his problem improved tremendously, but also that their connection with each other, their very relationship, had deepened: It was as if they could now communicate with each other effortlessly, not just on the ground, but also when riding. She also joked that she was comforted by the fact that even if she was pretty clueless, her horse was happy to step in and show her what to do.

This story illustrates Animal Reiki Lesson 4: Listen to your animal. In fact, you probably already do in many ways, but in the space of Reiki, you can learn to quiet your mind and truly just "be" with your animal. In that quiet space, you can begin to experience a new connection with your animal: a new understanding of his or her inner essence and spiritual being and ability to truly "listen" to what he or she has to say. Your new awareness will bring added depth and dimension to your relationship with each other, as well as shine a light on possibilities of connections with other animals that may cross your path in life!

Perhaps one of the most memorable lessons in all of my animal Reiki days involved deer: specifically, several deer, but in reality all are one.

It all began one October evening as my husband and I encountered a horrific scene: a beautiful young buck with little two-inch horns was being run over by an SUV just as we drove past. As I offered Reiki, I felt an immediate heat and "whoosh" of white light flood through my body. I also felt a sense of peace and understanding from the deer; for a moment his spirit had lingered on the street, not even realizing he had passed. With Reiki, he was carried gently and surely into the light. Although I knew Reiki had helped this deer, I felt overwhelmed by the difficult reality that deer face when living in the midst of human civilization. I could not erase the image of carnage from my mind. I wondered if I'd ever be able to sleep again without nightmares.

Later that night, as I walked my dog before bed, another buck, with identical little two-inch horns, stood in silent vigil across the street from my home. Although we had lived in that house for four years, we had never seen deer in our neighborhood. I was in awe and transfixed in his gaze. Then it dawned on me: It was as if he were a messenger come to say, "Have courage and hope." As soon as I had this thought, he turned away and walked slowly away into the mist. That night I slept peacefully, with the image of the healthy, young deer in my mind.

Just a few months later, a student of mine asked me to offer Reiki to a fawn whose mother had been hit and killed by the side of the highway. Wildlife volunteers and Animal Control were unable to catch the baby, and he refused to leave his mother's body. Everyone worried for his safety by the highway, his weakened state without food, and about what good outcome could possibly come from this. I felt a special connection to this situation, and remembered the two young bucks I had encountered a few months previously. As I began to offer Reiki to the mother's passing as well as the baby's situation, I knew that the perfect solution could be found (although I couldn't imagine what that could be). Courage and hope, I told myself. Just a few days later, my student contacted me to share unbelievable news: two young bucks had arrived out of nowhere, adopted the baby and taken her with them. The experts were amazed, as this was highly unusual, but they believed that with their help, the baby would be able to survive. Already anticipating the answer, I asked my student to describe the bucks. Sure enough, one of them had little two-inch horns.

This final story illustrates Animal Reiki Lesson 5: Always have courage and hope, no matter the situation. The hardest life lessons seem to always come in the form of transitions: the spirit's journey out of the body and on to the next chapter in existence. Working with Reiki and animals during this time is a way to embrace the process, both for the animal leaving his body and for the practitioner by his side. Despite how difficult it can be to work with animals who are dying, I have found that simply in this connection, there is no limit to the healing that can happen—on both sides. The animals have taught me always to remain positive. As this story shows, sometimes miracles do happen!

As you go through your daily life, open yourself to lessons from the animals around you. Remember that Reiki teachers come in all shapes and sizes, and all species, too! By their very natures, animals live in the energetic realm very freely and easily. They can sense and understand all kinds of subtle connections that are easily overlooked by humans.

Offering Reiki to animals can help us to become more aware not only of the wisdom of other species, but also of the energy that is all around you. And this new awareness, once experienced, can never be undone: It will transform the way you view Reiki possibilities for healing the world and all creatures in it.

CHAPTER TWENTY-FIVE

THE ANIMAL REIKI PRACTITIONER CODE OF ETHICS: SUPPORTING THE COMMITMENT OF TODAY'S PROFESSIONAL ANIMAL REIKI PRACTITIONER

Just a few years ago, it was nearly unheard of to find a Reiki practitioner whose practice was dedicated solely to animal clients. Today, there are hundreds of animal Reiki practitioners starting their businesses all over the world. In teaching so many of these enthusiastic and dedicated practitioners, I found myself motivated to bring together the animal Reiki community. Many of us have felt isolated, not only from the animal health field (as Reiki is just on the cusp of becoming well-known in holistic veterinary circles), but also from other Reiki practitioners, who often may ask us, "Working with animals is the same as working with people, isn't it?" Working with animals involves many of the same principles as working with people, but there are some additional factors that deserve mention, including our approach to the animals, our relationship with human companions, and art and nuance unique to the inter species Reiki dialog. A need began to present itself: a need to define and validate the uniqueness of the work that we do. A need to find a common ground from where to start as professional practitioners, and a language to express what it is that we do from our hearts for the animals—and something to help others know where we are coming from. And so, the Animal Reiki Practitioner Code of Ethics was born.

Before presenting the code itself, I'd like to share a few words about our commitment as animal Reiki practitioners—a commitment that begins with our own healing journey and moves outward to the animals, the animals' families, the animal health profession and the animal community itself. It is this inner commitment that motivates us in our mission not only to bring the wonderful healing of Reiki to the animals in our lives, but also, in doing so, to uphold the highest standards and protocols for our new and developing profession.

1. Commitment to Pursue a Healing Path for Ourselves and for the Animals.

Animal Reiki practitioners are committed to personal growth and healing through Reiki. We know that the more committed we are to our own personal practice of Reiki, the more effective we will be as healing channels for the animals. Thus, it is important to incorporate Reiki into our daily lives—to really "make it ours" in an authentic and unique way. The experience of Reiki in our own lives is in essence the experience of the healing that happens in the space of "Oneness." It is in this space that we realize we are not separate from the animals, that we can commune and connect with them at the deepest levels, and that we can view the world and its animals with compassion, reverence and gratitude. It is in this space that we find our heart's motivation to be truly committed to animal healing. As we work on our own issues, setting a daily intention for healing, we become clearer and stronger channels for Reiki healing. The animals will sense our pure intention to help them, as well as the energy we offer; it is amazing to see the animals come and ask for a treatment! It is a profound lesson in the intuitive depth of the animals, their energetic wisdom and the connection of all things at their very essence.

2. Commitment to Support the Animal's Family.

When we work with animals, we also work hand in hand with their animal companions. In addition, when animals are sick, injured or otherwise in need of healing, the whole family is affected (both animal and human members). Invite family members (human and animal) to sit in the room with you during the animal's treatment to absorb some Reiki as well. Sometimes human companions may even decide to set up a separate appointment for their own treatments.

There's another reason it's important to see yourself as supporting the whole family, not just the animal client: you are compassionately validating the significance and difficulty of caring for an injured, ill or dying animal, and the importance of the role the animal plays in the family. This is a validation often not echoed in our society. For example, many human companions of my clients have shared with me that when they went to work after their beloved animal companion had died, if they showed sadness or grief for more than a day or two, people would say things like, "It's only a dog (or cat, etc.). Get over it." Others have shared with me that when they decided to care for their animals despite chronic illness or disease, people would say, "That's a lot of work and expensive, too. Why don't you just put him down?" In bringing Reiki to the family, healing, peace and comfort will come to all aspects of the situation, including these.

If you are working with an animal who is very ill or approaching his or her transition, you can find yourself in a very emotional and stressful environment in the animal's home. Everyone in the family will be dealing with the situation differently, and it's important as the healing practitioner that you remain open and accepting of the feelings and needs of each family member. Staying centered and peaceful is important, as you can hold that vibration for everyone, creating a "healing space" in which everyone can feel comfortable to open themselves to the healing that Reiki offers.

Animal Reiki practitioners often receive intuitive information from the animal during treatment. This information may be helpful to the human companions in their understanding of what the animal is going through. In this case, it is good to share the information with them. It can provide comfort and clarity to the humans, which in turn brings stress relief to their animals. It's also important to remember not to overstep your bounds as the Reiki practitioner: Allow the human companions to find their own way, with the advice of a trusted veterinarian, in choosing the journey of the animal. For example, stay open, flexible and without judgment, even in the midst of difficult and emotional decisions, such as the decision to euthanize. Bringing Reiki to the situation will help things unfold in the best way for the animal.

3. Commitment to Support Other Animal Health Professionals and Needy Animals in the Community.

As allies to the veterinary profession, who are the leaders in our community when it comes to the health and well-being of our animals, we must work to create partnerships and cooperative relationships with both veterinarians and other practitioners in the animal health field. This can often be difficult since Reiki is still relatively unknown in the traditional veterinary profession and among many other animal health practitioners. It is important to see ourselves as working in tandem with not only vets, but also other supportive professionals such as animal chiropractors, animal acupuncture and acupressure practitioners, massage therapists, trainers, animal communicators, groomers, pet sitters and dog walkers. All of these people work toward the same goals: happiness, wellness and a good quality of life for our animal companions. Each animal's path to balance and wholeness may require a combination of many healing modalities, to which Reiki can be an integral and supportive component. Building professional alliances, sharing knowledge and creating friendships with other practitioners brings new knowledge, depth and insight from the wisdom of a multitude of healing disciplines to our own work. We can do so much more together than apart.

To further support the community, animal Reiki practitioners should reach out to the animals who need it most: those in shelters, sanctuaries and rescue centers. Many of us already donate our time and/or money to these organizations, and so in also bringing the gift of Reiki, we are simply stepping up to a new level of commitment to the needy animals of our community. In donating our time and knowledge for Reiki treatments for the animals and/or classes for the staff and volunteers of these facilities, we receive blessings and gifts from the animals we are helping that outweigh our efforts many times over. Many of Reiki's deepest lessons in animal healing are to be found within the walls of your neighborhood animal shelter, or tucked away behind the fence of your nearby animal sanctuary. In addition, in becoming a valued volunteer to these organizations, we build community friendships that will last a lifetime.

4. Commitment to Educate Others About Animal Reiki.

We are by nature pioneers in this work in the holistic animal health field, and so must learn to educate other animal health professionals and veterinarians about what we do (even if we are not at first comfortable with being "educators"), so that they can understand the value of integrating Reiki into the animal's healing program. This education extends to the human companions of the animals with whom we work: We must learn to create a language about what we do so that humans feel comfortable in letting us treat their "fur kids." This includes explaining what they should expect a treatment to look like and common behavioral reactions to the energy. It also involves letting them know that the animal, not the Reiki practitioner, is in charge of exactly how (and indeed whether) the treatment unfolds.

Luckily, in addition to the words of our own explanations to people about Reiki with animals, the experience of the treatment speaks even more powerfully than anything we ourselves can say. The animals, so wise and well-versed in the language of energy already (as is their nature), show us clearly in their physical, mental, emotional and spiritual responses not only that they feel the energy of Reiki, but also that they benefit greatly from it. Yes, the animals are often the best Reiki teachers—a lesson learned best when accessed from a place of humility and respect, where the animals are active partners in the process.

We are also pioneers in the Reiki world, as most practitioners have trained and work solely or primarily with humans. Our human-client counterparts are often very interested in the differences in approach and method when working with animals. We can learn from their human treatment experiences. In addition, sharing lessons the animals have taught us can benefit every Reiki practitioner; we can gain insights into Reiki treatments, the profound nature of the healing process, the universal language of energy, as well as life lessons in courage, joy, hope, forgiveness and gratitude, just to name a few.

The Animal Reiki Code of Ethics
Developed by Kathleen Prasad

Guiding Principles:

* I believe the animals are equal partners in the healing process.
* I honor the animals as being not only my clients, but also my teachers in the journey of healing.
* I understand that all animals have physical, mental, emotional and spiritual aspects, to which Reiki can bring profound healing responses.
* I believe that bringing Reiki to the human/animal relationship is transformational to the human view of the animal kingdom.
* I dedicate myself to the virtues of humility, integrity, compassion and gratitude in my Reiki practice.

In working on myself, I follow these practices:

* I incorporate the Five Reiki Precepts into my daily life and Reiki practice.
* I commit myself to a daily practice of self-healing and spiritual development so that I can be a clear and strong channel for healing energy.
* I nurture a belief in the sacred nature of all beings, and in the value and depth of animalkind as our partners on this planet.

- I listen to the wisdom of my heart, remembering that we are all One.

In working with the animals, I follow these guidelines:

- I work in partnership with the animal.
- I always ask permission of the animal before beginning, and respect his or her decision to accept or refuse any treatment. I listen intuitively and observe the animal's body language in determining the response.
- I allow each animal to choose how to receive his or her treatment; thus each treatment could be a combination of hands-on, short distance and/or distant healing, depending on the animal's preference.
- I let go of my expectations about how the treatment should progress and/or how the animal should behave during the treatment, and simply trust Reiki.
- I accept the results of the treatment without judgment and with gratitude toward Reiki and the animal's openness and participation in the process.

In working with the human companions of the animals, I will:

- Share information before the treatment about my healing philosophy, the Reiki healing system and what to expect in a typical treatment, as well as possible outcomes, including the possibility of healing reactions.
- Provide a clear policy ahead of time regarding fees, length of treatment and cancellation policy, as well as "postponement" policy, should the animal not want the treatment that day.
- Never diagnose. I will always refer clients to a licensed veterinarian when appropriate.
- Honor the privacy of the animals and their human companions.
- Share intuition received during Reiki treatments, with compassion and humility, for the purpose of supporting their understanding of the healing process.
- Respect the human companion's right to choose the animal's healing journey, selecting the methods, both holistic and/or conventional that he or she deems most appropriate, with the support and advice of a trusted veterinarian.

In working in the community, I hold the following goals:

- I model the values of partnership, compassion, humility, gentleness and gratitude in my life and with the animals, teaching by example.
- I work to create professional alliances and cooperative relationships with other Reiki practitioners/teachers, animal health-care providers and animal welfare organizations in my community.
- I strive to educate my community in its understanding of the benefits of Reiki for animals.
- I continually educate myself to maintain and enhance my professional competence so that I uphold the integrity of the profession.
- I consider myself an ally to the veterinary and animal health community. I work to support their efforts in achieving animal wellness and balance. I honor other disciplines and their practitioners.

CHAPTER TWENTY-SIX

HEALING BEYOND WORDS WITH ANIMAL REIKI

Breathing in, I calm body and mind. Breathing out, I smile. Dwelling in the present moment I know this is the only moment. -Thich Nhat Hanh

Each lifelong relationship between an animal and his person is a unique heart-to-heart dance: elegant, graceful and flowing. To be able to be present with an open heart is a beautiful gift. To be able to support animals and their people—to hold a meditative space of compassion, peace and love in that moment whatever it looks like—happy, sad, hopeful or uncertain—this is the true highest calling of the animal Reiki practitioner.

Healing Beyond Language

When I started doing Reiki, I was very interested in animal communication, and it was a big piece of what I wanted to do. I think you can feel that in my first book, those of you who've read Animal Reiki. A lot of the stories are about the communications I received from the animals. In the beginning, when I was doing treatments with the animals, I was really focusing on messages that I could share with the people. In certain times and situations, I think these messages can be helpful. However, things have changed a lot for me over fifteen years of practice.

I still experience communication in the way of animals teaching me. I want to be open and listening, and there's a beautiful heart connection there. But I feel that Reiki goes even deeper.

The foundation for all my work with the animals is my own personal, meditative, spiritual practice. I find the place that is most healing for myself, is also the place to which animals are most drawn. It is a place without words and without judgments: that deep quiet space where language has no meaning. So now, and what's been my focus for the last eight years or so, I work on letting go: letting go of my mind, of my impressions, of my judgments and of my interpretations. Letting go, letting go, letting go.

> *You should therefore cease from practice based on intellectual understanding, pursuing words and following after speech, and learn the backward step that turns your light inwardly to illuminate your self.* -Dogen

Layers of Existence

> *We shape clay into a pot, but it is the emptiness inside that holds whatever we want.* -Tao Te Ching

Imagine an animal's being, essence and spirit as a beautiful sphere of light. The outer layer of the sphere would be the physical part. Any ailments we see, behaviors, all the things we see with our eyes are in this outer layer. And if we go deeper into that sphere, just under the surface, we find the mental/emotional aspects of the animal that we can't really see with our eyes, unless it's reflected in the behavior. Sometimes we can see it, but sometimes it's very subtle. We need to be good listeners and in tune with our intuition to pick up on deeper physical issues as well as emotional/mental aspects of animals.

If we go even deeper, we can connect to the spiritual aspect of the animal. The spiritual aspect is that inner light which is your animal's deepest, purest essence. It is housed for a time on this earth in this body, but it is eternal. It existed before the animal came into this world, as a dog, cat or horse. It stays for this lifetime. Then the body may pass away, but the light continues. This light just "is." It is the inner most essence of the animals, of you, of me, of the mountains, the sky, the sun and the moon. All things consist in their deepest essence of this light. In other words, when we access our true spiritual nature, we access our non-dual aspect, our connection to the whole, to our oneness. In this space there are no words.

It's that deep, energetic, eternal core of being that is touched with Reiki-and our most important healing potential and self-healing power resides there, within the space of compassion and love. When we share compassion with the spiritual essence of ourselves or another being, healing automatically manifests, and the ripple effects can be seen in the mental, emotional and physical layers of being, and this is why we can often see such beautiful healing shifts after practicing Reiki.

Communication often deals with the layers outside of the spiritual layer: the mental/emotional and physical layers that are more connected with this lifetime's journey. And in order to be successful at communication, we have to practice focusing on what we can pick up and then interpret and express it to the animal's people. So we are working with a layer just below the surface. Sometimes we can also dip into the spiritual, however communication limits our ability to go deeply into this layer because it requires a dualistic frame of reference in order to interpret and express through language.

With Reiki, we can transcend the limits and boundaries of language, even melt away the differences of species, and in this open space, miracles of healing can happen!

Accessing Inner Wisdom and Clarity

In addition to the healing power of connection in the Reiki space, I find that in my work with animals' people, it's much more powerful if an animal's person can discover wisdom and clarity about his animal for himself. To have that "light bulb moment" is very transformative. It is much more powerful than me telling someone something that I intuited. Maybe the person isn't ready to hear it, maybe the way I express it is not the best way and the person gets offended, or maybe it could cause worry or upset. We have to be so careful when we express something that we "got" during a treatment.

What I find more profound than me interpreting an animal's message for a person, is going deeper, resisting the allure of language, judgment and interpretation, and simply holding a space of healing for the animal-and I always include the family of the animal (both humans and non-humans) in that treatment. Reiki can create a space of wisdom and clarity for all so that when they are ready and at the perfect moment, they can realize all that they need to know, coming to that conclusion for themselves, knowing it for themselves from a very deep place. When wisdom comes to us in this kind of way, internally and authentically, at the right moment, then it really "sticks" and creates a profound shift in our inner being.

Is it possible for anyone to realize inner wisdom and clarity? I believe that we already know everything we need to know to make the right decisions for our animals and ourselves. But sometimes our emotions get in the way so that we feel muddy and can't clearly know what our animal wants and needs. But I believe that when we love an animal, or when we open our heart in compassion to an animal, our deepest heart and spirit has touched the animal's deepest heart and spirit, and in this connection there is a deep wisdom, which only has to be brought to the surface. Reiki can create the space where this can happen.

As Reiki practitioners, everything that we pick up goes through our own filters, life experience, opinions and feelings. We can get easily off-track when we try to interpret and judge these things. Communication can become a distraction. By trusting and letting go into the Reiki space, we nurture that space of the spirit where all kinds of issues shift and resolve into a space of clarity, wisdom, peace and healing-without words, without conversation, without interpretation.

Patience with the Process

Communication can sometimes be helpful and supportive. Maybe we have received an intuitive message from a gifted person and it resonated and made a difference for us. I believe that's because our spirit already knew it to be true, and our emotional and physical bodies were processing it-in other words we were already there anyway! But sometimes, even if we are able to share an intuitive message that may be accurate, I see all the time that people may not be ready to hear it. They may be too angry, not ready to let go and heal, etc. So then the message either falls on deaf ears or causes more anger or worry or guilt. Or maybe we do understand what the communicator is saying intellectually, but emotionally we just aren't quite there yet.

We can often see this with animals who may be dying and the people aren't ready to let them go. It doesn't do any good for the Reiki practitioner to say, "You know what, you need to let them go. This isn't about you, it's about the animal." Even if it's true and we find a nice way to say it, still, the people may not be ready to accept this. Or the people may agree intellectually but not be able to do it emotionally and then feel terrible and guilty, and have a big heaviness from our words on top of everything else they are going through.

I know I found this for myself in my own journey towards my dog's transition—I understood intellectually what needed to happen long before my emotional body was ready to be on board with the letting go. Lots of layers, grieving, resistance, control, anger, sadness, all of it-needed to be worked through before I could say, with all of my mind and emotions, "It's ok for you to go; I will be ok." So much healing needed to happen within me before I could really feel the authenticity of those words through my entire being. Reiki helped me to get there.

As Reiki practitioners, we have no agenda, no time pressure, no forcing or fixing-we can simply "be" with the person and the animal. With our open heart and compassionate presence, we can see attitudes, situations and emotions all shift towards balance, understanding and acceptance. Be patient and just "be" with Reiki, and healing will happen!

The Power of Compassionate Presence

Whatever the problem, Reiki speaks louder than words to support the healing process. Reiki practitioners can bring compassionate presence to the ups and downs of any healing situation. Reiki practitioners can be supportive listeners and witnesses, always remaining peaceful and grounded. Even through the hard parts, when people are in denial or get angry and frustrated, Reiki practitioners just hold the space-gently, openly and without judgment. To be able to sit in a grounded, peaceful space through all of that heavy emotion-without getting knocked over by it-this is a beautiful gift we can offer to animals and their people, and to ourselves. Reiki can bring about transformational healing, love and acceptance. Yes, I have seen it again and again and again.

Reiki also nurtures the empowerment of the animal and their people. In the Reiki space which is beyond language, beyond interpretation, where there is no conversation or discussion—in that deeper place resides true compassion, the capacity to access our deepest wisdom and true miracles of healing potential. That's the place I want to nurture inside myself, for my own healing, and for the animals, for their healing. I want to dig deep into Reiki and then just let go into that quiet space. How do we get to that place? There is no shortcut; we just have to practice. Practice every day, for the rest of your life.

CHAPTER TWENTY-SEVEN

REIJU AND ANIMALS: WHEN, HOW, AND MOST IMPORTANTLY, WHY?

We need another and a wiser and perhaps a more mystical concept of animals... In a world older and more complete than ours they move finished and complete, gifted with extensions of the senses we have lost or never attained, living by voices we shall never hear. They are not brethren, they are not underlings; they are other nations, caught with ourselves in the net of life and time, fellow prisoners of the splendor and travail of the earth.

This quote by Henry Beston illustrates an important point about animals which should be considered when discussing Reiki initiations/attunements/Reiju. (For the purposes of this article, I will use the terms initiation, attunement and Reiju interchangeably.) We must remember that their energetic sensitivities and abilities far exceed ours. This is not because they "practice" (as we must), but rather because it simply is WHO they are, in their bodies on this earth. They are tuned into the language of energy: comfortably fluent and fluid in its ebbs and flows, while we humans must struggle, focus and practice to sense this subtle layer of existence.

There exists lots of confusion surrounding Reiki and initiating animals. For example, I've heard some people describing their animals as Reiki Level 1 or 2, or even a "Reiki Master" based solely on receiving an initiation. It seems to me that Reiki levels and the ritual aspect of the system have no meaning or importance for animals. And yet animals do love to connect with us through Reiki and benefit from it as well. In this article, I'd like to share a little bit about the ways I believe animals connect with us in the Reiki space along with some considerations one should make before giving his/her animal a Reiki initiation.

Consideration 1: State of Mind—The Precepts

The most important element of Mikao Usui's teachings is resting our mind on the precepts, so that we can lead a life without anger and worry, and therefore we can be humble, honest and compassionate. All the rest of the teachings, (hands on healing, meditations, symbols/mantras, Reiju) are tools to help us to be in that state of mind.

This quote by my teacher Frans Stiene is at the root of the discussion about Reiki initiations and animals. In my opinion, the most successful connections between animals and people within the Reiki space (whether we are talking about treatments, meditations, or Reiju) happen because we attain a correct state of mind. It is the precepts that serve as our guide and foundation. When we are in a peaceful, compassionate state, without anger, fear, ego or judgment, our energy rests. It becomes still, stable, calm. It radiates serenity. The animals sense this and are drawn forward to connect with us. On the other hand, animals also sense when our energy is disturbed (for example by anger, worry, judgment or ego) and may say "no" to connecting with us. So our state of mind will often determine whether or not an animal will choose to share Reiki (treatment, meditation, or Reiju) with us.

Consideration 2: Practice and Letting Go of Ego

When offering Reiki to animals, I would say that one of the most important qualities we should nurture in ourselves is a letting go of ego. As Frans says, "It is extremely difficult to completely step out of the way—our ego has such a strong grip on everything. This is why the *system* of Reiki is a spiritual and lifelong practice."

One key point in this quote is that our personal practice is the real foundation of our work with the animals. It is what will give us the trust and courage that we need to stay stable, strong, grounded and calm no matter what issues we may face when supporting an animal and his family. The precepts, the symbols and mantras, the meditations, the Reiju: practicing all of these elements supports our ability to connect with the animals through treatments. Similarly, each element of the system of Reiki supports the other elements and helps them function successfully as tools for our self-development, like pieces of a perfect and clever puzzle.

The other key point in the quote regards ego; if we can practice letting go of our ego, than it no longer matters that "I am human, you are dog (cat, horse, etc.)." Connecting with animals and Reiki can help us to realize that our species differences are just on the surface, that at our essence we are all one. In this space of oneness we can realize that perhaps it is the animals who will teach us; perhaps it is they who will offer the healing space for us. If we are in a space of ego, ("I am the elevated human, you are the lowly animal. You need me!") then we are not in a space of listening where we can hear what the animals are telling us about what they need and want from us during Reiki. In fact, we may receive resistance from the animals with whom we are trying to connect. And even worse, we might miss the most beautiful gifts of healing that they are willing to share with us because we just aren't willing to listen.

Consideration 3: Movement (Ritual) vs. Stillness (State of Mind)

Here is a key difference in offering Reiki to animals versus people. People usually need the ritual of movement and touch to help them to connect with energy, while animals prefer connecting from a deeper place, more of a mind-to-mind or heart-to-heart connection. For example, when you visualize the human Reiki treatment, you can picture the client lying on a massage table, while the practitioner moves around him or her, using hand positions on or off the body. The overall dynamic here is that the client is basically still, while the practitioner moves, following a sort of physical ritual.

In an animal Reiki treatment, on the other hand, it's best for the practitioner to sit or stand in the center of the space, remaining quiet, still and meditative while holding an open state of mind. Physical ritual can disturb an animal's sensibilities, and so animal treatments are most successful when the practitioner can drop the ritual and turn his focus inward. While the practitioner holds this space, the animal will then move around the person, sometimes coming forward to receive hands-on contact, sometimes moving farther away. Occasionally the practitioner might move in sync with the animal, for example in horse treatments where a mirroring of movement is often seen, a Reiki "dance" of sorts. But even in this case, it is the animal who guides the movement, not the practitioner.

So we can say that while movement most often characterizes animal acceptance of Reiki, it is stillness that most often characterizes people's acceptance of Reiki. And on the other hand, it is the ritual that is most often preferred as practitioner behavior in human treatment; it is the state of mind in the practitioner which helps animal treatment to succeed.

In both the cases of humans and animals, the Reiki practitioner will use intuition to determine where and whether hands-on contact will be used, however in a human treatment, the client wouldn't usually come forward and guide this part of the treatment, mostly just because we humans are pretty unaware of the subtleties of energy. Animals on the other hand can sense the energy quite easily, moving into and out of its flow at will; in other words, animals know how to take charge of the treatment in their own way. Their deeper knowledge of energy guides us, the practitioners. They often show us just what to do, or more to the point, how to "be."

Consideration 4: The Human Paradigm

Although the above description describes Reiki treatment, it is important to consider this difference in regards to initiating animals— whether and why we should or shouldn't do it. On the one hand, you could say that a Reiju is simply a spiritual blessing, and so of course all beings would benefit from them for this reason. But then we need to look at the ritual aspect of this blessing. After all, wouldn't the physical aspect of Reiju require the animal to be still, while the practitioner moved around them, following a specified pattern of movements? So asking an animal to sit still for an attunement is similar to asking them to hop onto a massage table while we "do" the treatment.

As in animal Reiki treatment, when if/when we are offering an initiation to an animal, it is our state of mind which will create that space. If we come from an egoistic state of "doing," (focusing on the physical ritual) most animals will resist or walk away from connection. Even if we manage to hold an egoless state of mind, animals rarely conform to the paradigm of "animal motionless/practitioner moving." And so, if we return to the example of treatment dynamic we can see that simply by performing physical ritual "on" the animal, we are asking them to submit to a situation that is not naturally preferred. And so therein lies the problem.

Frans says, "Reiju, hands on healing, distance healing, initiation, symbols, mantras, meditation, life, the precepts, attunement, you name it, are all one and the same when we start to tap into our true nature, no difference at all." Why would we perform the ritual of Reiju, asking the animals to conform to our human paradigm, when in essence, if we are in the right space, the right state of mind, we could create just as healing of a space for them as if we simply offered them a Reiki treatment. So the key here really is, as Frans illuminates, to tap into our true nature; and when we do this, species differences melt away and profound interspecies connections are forged.

Wouldn't it be better to meet the animal on his or her own terms, to allow them to move, to keep our physical body calm and in a non-dominant pose, simply sitting quietly in an open and connected state of mind? Then we can simply invite them to share the healing space. In reality, this is the true Reiju we can give to the animals: being present, flexible, open and accepting of their unique ways of being while dropping all separateness and becoming one.

Consideration 5: Who is Teaching Whom?

One of the principles of a Reiju, is that the teacher offering it, presumably has more experience than the student. Well, in the case of animals, clearly the animals are more at home in the world of energy, more attuned to its finer points, more aware of its healing properties. So then I wonder—if we have a human and an animal in the room, and someone should be giving an initiation, perhaps it should be the animal giving it to the person. Of course I am saying this tongue in cheek (since these kinds of rituals have no meaning for animals) however the principle still I think is important. The more that we can come from a place of humility in our approach with animals, the better our Reiki responses from them will be. In addition, although personally I've never been drawn to offer the ritual of Reiju to an animal, I've experienced many times that beautiful space of openness and oneness with the animals, something that, yes, I would describe as a spiritual blessing (without the ritual). Even more, I have had the beautiful privilege of having animals come forward and assist me when I am offering or teaching Reiju to people.

Recently I was teaching a Level 3 Reiki class, and the students were practicing initiations on each other. As I stood there, guiding the students and holding the space, one of the resident cats at BrightHaven, Rosie, ran into the room, jumped onto the table beside me and meowed plaintively. Clearly she wanted me to pick her up immediately! I lifted her into my arms and held her for the duration of the initiation practice as she cuddled against my chest. It's difficult to describe the wonderful feeling of communion, her feline purring heart against my quiet human heart, while I held an open space for the students. Connecting with her

during the sacred ritual of Reiju created within me a feeling of spiritual expansion and connectedness to the whole, yet at the same time being totally physical in my body, grounded and present. She was supporting me to be a better facilitator for my students at that moment!

In fact, not only in Reiju, but also in all the elements of Reiki, I believe animals help us to be in a better, more open and receptive place to receive the benefits of our practice and to go deeper into the space of connection. Contemplating the precepts, meditating, chanting, doing treatments and performing Reiju are all, in my opinion, practices that can be even more beneficial and enjoyable when done in the presence of an animal.

So in conclusion, if you are feeling the urge to perform the physical ritual of Reiju on your animal, be sure to ask yourself—is this really for your animal or is it for you?

APPENDIX

FINAL THOUGHTS ON BECOMING THE BEST PRACTITIONER YOU CAN BE

"Your Reiki Journey Begins Here..."

Make Reiki a regular part of your life; immerse yourself in the practice.

The animals will be your guides and teachers.

Do self-healing every day.

Treat another being every day (plant, person or animal).

Get Reiki treatments when you can.

Give back to the planet; volunteer Reiki regularly at a shelter, sanctuary, or other animal place in need.

WHAT ARE YOU WAITING FOR?

Heal Yourself And Your Animals Today With Reiki!

MEDITATION

- 🐾 reduces stress
- 🐾 reduces anxiety
- 🐾 relieves depression
- 🐾 relieves pain

BENEFITS OF ANIMAL REIKI

ANIMAL THERAPY

- 🐾 reduces stress
- 🐾 relieves depression
- 🐾 provides companionship
- 🐾 relieves feelings of isolation

HEALING TOUCH

- 🐾 relieves pain
- 🐾 reduces stress
- 🐾 reduces fatigue
- 🐾 relieves depression
- 🐾 reduces anxiety

For more information visit **www.animalreikisource.com**

ANIMAL Reiki source

CONTINUING EDUCATION AND SUPPORT FROM ANIMAL REIKI SOURCE

Teleclasses

(Please visit Animal Reiki Source for a list of in person and online learning opportunities - http://animalreikisource.com/reiki-classes)

- Reiki for Dogs

- Introduction to Animal Reiki

- Animals and the Elements Teleclass Series

- The Animal Reiki Workshop: Core Curriculum

- Private Consultations/Teaching Sessions (by appointment only)

Correspondence Learning

(http://animalreikisource.com/reiki-classes/animal-reiki-workshop-core-curriculum-correspondence)

- The Animal Reiki Workshop: Core Curriculum

Audio Courses

(http://animalreikisource.com/reiki-classes/animal-reiki-audio-courses)

- The Medicine Buddha Chant

- The Reiki 1 Audio Course

- Reiki for Dogs

- Animal Healing Meditations

- Finding Your Center: Healing the Animals of the World by Going Within

- Healing Fearful Animals with Reiki

- Series of Species-specific Animal Reiki Audios

- To Touch or not to Touch? Physical Contact, Human Intuition and the Animal Reiki Treatment

- Reiki, Animal Hospice and Transitions: How Practitioners Can Best Support the Process

Support and Inspiration

- Animal Reiki Talk: the first Tuesday of every month by teleconference (*animalreikisource.com/reiki-classes/animal-reiki-talk*)

- Animal Reiki Source Yahoo Group (*http://pets.groups.yahoo.com/group/animalreikisource/*)

- Animal Reiki Source Newsletter Sign Up *(sign up at www.animalreikisource.com)*

- Animal Reiki Source Facebook (*https://www.facebook.com/AnimalReikiSource*)

- Animal Reiki Source Twitter (*https://twitter.com/ars_animalreiki*)

- Animal Reiki Source YouTube Channel (*https://www.youtube.com/user/AnimalReikiSource*)

- Kathleen Prasad's Blog – It's a Heartful Life (*http://www.itsaheartfullife.com/*)

- Shelter Animal Reiki Association (*http://www.shelteranimalreikiassociation.org/*)

- Shelter Animal Reiki Association Blog
  (http://www.shelteranimalreikiassociation.org/blog/)

- Shelter Animal Reiki Association Facebook
  (https://www.facebook.com/ShelterAnimalReikiAssociation)

- Shelter Animal Reiki Association Twitter
  (https://twitter.com/sara_news)

- Shelter Animal Reiki Association YouTube Channel
  (https://www.youtube.com/user/ShelterReiki)

- Frans Stiene of the International House of Reiki Facebook
  (https://www.facebook.com/frans.stiene)

- Frans Stiene of the International House of Reiki Google+
  (https://plus.google.com/110583548752979372458/posts)

RECOMMENDED READING/RESOURCES

Animal Reiki Books

Healing Virtues: Transforming Your Practice Through the Animal Reiki Code of Ethics, by Kathleen Prasad, Animal Reiki Source, 2017.

> An in-depth guide on the best and most ethical ways to share Reiki with animals. Because ethical practice is the most important obligation of an animal Reiki practitioner, this book should be required reading for all Reiki practitioners working with animals.

Heart To Heart With Horses: The Equine Lover's Guide to Reiki, by Kathleen Prasad, Animal Reiki Source, 2016.

> Real-life stories, inspiring case studies and simple Reiki meditative exercises show how easy it is to share the gift of true healing with the horses you love.

How to Help Animals with Reiki, by Kathleen Prasad, Kindle, 2015.

> This book includes numerous guidelines and tips for treatments, information about how animals teach us about healing, why an open state of mind is so important when we approach animals with Reiki, and how to use things like patience, positivity, intuition and physical touch to help put animals at ease for optimum responses.

Reiki for Dogs, by Kathleen Prasad, Ulysses Press, 2012.

> Full of information, tips, case studies and both new and traditional meditations to help you connect more deeply with the dogs (and other animals) in your life.

The Animal Reiki Handbook: Finding Your Way with Reiki in Your Local Shelter, Sanctuary or Rescue, Kathleen Prasad and SARA Members, Shelter Animal Reiki Association, 2009.

> This book is a comprehensive guide to using Reiki with all species of animals in shelter/sanctuary/rescue settings.

Tails from the Source: The Animal Reiki Source Newsletter Collection, Volume I, 2004-2005, edited by Kathleen Prasad, Lulu Press, 2008.

> This book is a collection of case studies from Animal Reiki practitioners around the world. Included are stories of the transformational power of Reiki in the lives of many species of animals.

Animal Reiki: Using Energy to Heal the Animals in Your Life, Elizabeth Fulton and Kathleen Prasad, Ulysses Press, 2006.

> The first book of its kind, devoted solely to Reiki and animals, including special chapters focusing on treatment of different species. Includes "how-to" information along with real life stories of animal healing from the authors' experiences.

Reiki Books

The Inner Heart of Reiki – Rediscovering Your True Self, Frans Stiene

> This book will awaken readers to the deeper possibilities of their Reiki practice and offers techniques to help them get there.

The Reiki Sourcebook, Revised and Expanded, Bronwen and Frans Stiene

> One of the most comprehensive books on the system of Reiki ever published, this book will become an invaluable asset for Reiki novices, students and teachers alike.

The Japanese Art of Reiki, Bronwen and Frans Stiene

> More detailed and structured meditative techniques with a "Martial Arts" bent.

Audio Reiki Meditations in CD and/or mp3 Format

Medicine Buddha Chant, Kathleen Prasad
(http://www.animalreikisource.com/reiki-classes/-medicine-buddha-chant)

> Created to support the healing of people and their animals. Visit the site referenced above for more information and to listen to a sample of the audio.

Animal Healing Meditations, Kathleen Prasad
(http://www.animalreikisource.com/reiki-store/animal-healing-meditations)

> Kathleen created this meditation audio especially for you and your animals. The meditations will help you to tune into and connect energetically with your animals, with the natural world around you and with that deep inner space of peace and strength within yourself. It is this inner peace and strength that you can draw upon when your animal is facing any kind of healing challenge—be it physical, mental, emotional or spiritual. These meditations come from her book *Reiki for Dogs*, however the meditations for this audio can be used with animals of any species.

Five Power Animal Meditations Course: A Guided Journey to Strengthen Your Connection to Animal Wisdom, Kathleen Prasad
(http://www.animalreikisource.com/reiki-store/5-power-animal-meditations-course)

> Kathleen has created this meditation course for all animal lovers interested in making an inward journey towards energetic and spiritual connections to the wisdom of animal kind. The animals focused on in this course include the wolf, the tiger, the elephant, the bear and the eagle.

Primordial Sounds for Healing, Frans Stiene
(http://www.amazon.com/Primordial-Sounds-Healing-Frans-Stiene/dp/B00DBQoDRU)

Meditation from a Zen Perspective

Zen Mind, Beginner's Mind, Shunryu Suzuki

Not Always So, Shunryu Suzuki

Branching Streams Flow in the Darkness, Shunryu Suzuki

Being Peace, Thich Nhat Hanh

Teachings of the Earth: Zen and the Environment, John Dado Loori

Cave of Tigers: The Living Zen Practice, John Dado Loori

The Demon's Sermon on the Martial Arts, William Scott Wilson

The Art of Peace, Morihei Ueshiba and John Stevens

A New Earth, Eckhart Tolle

Animal Books

The Brighthaven Resource Guide, Gail and Richard Pope

Peace, Hope and Hospice, Gail Pope

Blessing the Bridge: What Animals Teach Us About Death Dying and Beyond, Rita M. Reynolds

Four Paws, Five Directions – A Guide to Chinese Medicine for Cats and Dogs, Cheryl Schwartz and Mark Ed. Schwartz

Natural Health Bible for Dogs and Cats, Shawn Messonnier, DVM

The Faraway Horses: The Adventures and Wisdom of One of America's Most Renowned Horsemen, Buck Brannaman and Bill Reynolds

Unexpected Miracles: Hope and Holistic Healing for Pets

The Emotional Lives of Animals: A Leading Scientist Explores Animal Joy, Sorrow and Empathy—and Why They Matter, Marc Bekoff, Ph.D. and Jane Goodall

Why Dogs Hump and Bees Get Depressed, Marc Bekoff, Ph.D.

The Animal Manifesto: Six Reasons for Expanding Our Compassion Footprint, Marc Bekoff, Ph.D.

Down to Earth Natural Horse Care, Lisa Ross-Williams

Dogs Never Lie About Love, Jeffrey Moussaieff Masson

Love, Life and Elephants: An African Love Story, Daphne Sheldrick

Kids Books

A Garden of Whales, Maggie Davis and Jennifer O'Connell

The Quiltmakers Gift, Jeff Brumbeau and Gail de Marcken

The Quiltmakers Journey, Jeff Brumbeau and Gail de Marcken

The Boy Who Grew Flowers, Jen Wojtowicz and Steve Adams

Tarra & Bella: The Elephant and Dog Who Became Best Friends, Carol Buckley

Owen & Mzee: The True Story of a Remarkable Friendship, Isabella Hatkoff and Craig Hatkoff

Urashima Taro and Other Japanese Children's Favorite Stories, Florence Sakade and Yoshio Hayashi

The Three Questions, Jon J. Muth

Time for Bed, Mem Fox and Jane Dyer

IF YOU LIKED THIS BOOK, TAKE THE COURSE!

This book is based on a three day course called "Everything Animal Reiki" which Kathleen Prasad teaches a few times a year in a variety of locations. In order to experience a deeper understanding of the teachings in this book, Kathleen recommends that students travel to take an in-person course with her.

Praise

The classes are casual, informative, and often emotional. Kathleen's years of experience and dedication to animals and Reiki shine through. Her warmth is captivating.-Karen H., CA

This class far, far surpassed my expectations. I thought I'd just learn how to use my Reiki training to help the animals in my life but it was so much more. It touched that place deep down inside of me that speaks to my soul. I felt truly blessed by this experience. Kathleen is a gifted teacher who really shares her bliss. The animals of this world are so lucky to have her sharing her Reiki and her devotion to their well being. -Trish H., CA

Animal Reiki has given me the language of universal communication necessary to help every situation for the highest good and the knowledge that now I am helping to heal all the levels of disharmony within the animals I treat. -Patricia J., DVM

For more information on attending the next session of "Everything Animal Reiki!" please visit www.AnimalReikiSource.com.

IN GRATITUDE ...

I would like to offer a special thank you to Frans Stiene for his continuing research into Reiki's historical origins and his dedication to the energetic practice of the system.

Special thanks also to the amazing team who helped make this book a reality:

Leah D'Ambrosio: Production
Sheryl Schlameuss: Design
Hiroko Sasanuki: Calligraphy

ABOUT THE SHELTER ANIMAL REIKI ASSOCIATION (SARA)

reiki to the rescue

SARA's founding principles are:

Passion - Commitment - Service

The mission of the Shelter Animal Reiki Association (SARA) is to improve the lives of animals and their caretakers by promoting the use of Reiki meditation in animal shelters, sanctuaries and rescues worldwide through education, training, specialized research and the advancement of Reiki programs that meet the highest standards of integrity and professionalism.

SARA is a 501(c)3 nonprofit that supports:

- health and wellness of animals in shelters, sanctuaries and rescues.
- caregivers at each animal organization.

Through Reiki treatment and training programs, SARA educates:

- interested shelter, sanctuary and rescue staff and caregivers.
- interested veterinarians.
- animal lovers in the community at large.

SARA seeks to promote Reiki's standing in the scientific community by:

- supporting ethical and animal-friendly animal Reiki research studies.
- creating alliances with the veterinary community.

Through SARA's ongoing professional development, training and evaluation program for members, SARA seeks to:

- promote the highest standards in Animal Reiki Practitioner and Teacher excellence.
- provide ongoing support for Animal Reiki Practitioners and Teachers volunteering in shelters, sanctuaries and rescues.

If each of us does his or her small part for the animals in our lives, imagine how those little acts of compassion can build up and grow all around the world. –Kathleen Prasad, Reiki for Dogs

SARA is dedicated to the memory of Dakota, Kathleen Prasad's beloved dog and the inspiration for Kathleen's work in the field of animal Reiki.

Visit SARA's website at www.shelteranimalreikiassociation.org for more information, merchandise and to make a tax-deductible donation.

ABOUT THE AUTHOR

Kathleen Prasad is founder of Animal Reiki Source and president of the 501(c)3 nonprofit Shelter Animal Reiki Association (SARA). She has taught Reiki meditative wellness techniques to thousands of animal lovers around the world, as well as the staff and volunteers of organizations such as BrightHaven, The CARE Foundation, Remus Memorial Horse Sanctuary, Best Friends Animal Society, The San Francisco SPCA and Guide Dogs for the Blind.

Kathleen has authored the books *Reiki for Dogs, How to Help Animals With Reiki* and *5 Powerful Meditations to Help Heal Your Animals* and co-authored the books: *The Animal Reiki Handbook* and *Animal Reiki: Using Energy to Heal the Animals in Your Life.* She's been published in magazines such as *The Journal of the American Holistic Veterinary Medical Association, Animal Wellness Magazine, Animal Fair, Equine Wellness Magazine, The Whole Dog Journal, Dog Fancy, Feline Wellness* and *Dogs Naturally Magazine,* and featured in several radio and TV programs. Considered the world expert in this field, as well as a dynamic speaker and passionate advocate for spiritual wellness of animals and their people, she has been invited to England, France and Australia to teach and speak about Reiki for Animals. Kathleen offers courses around the country as well as regular classes at BrightHaven Holistic Animal Retreat in Santa Rosa. She also teaches a variety of correspondence and tele-classes.

Made in the USA
Las Vegas, NV
27 April 2023

71196542R00079